W9-BWK-297

FRIENDS
OF ACPL

MAY 17 '67

# I Passed

# as a

# Teenager

## by LYN TORNABENE

### Simon and Schuster
### New York

All rights reserved
including the right of reproduction
in whole or in part in any form
Copyright © 1967 by Lyn Tornabene
Published by Simon and Schuster
Rockefeller Center, 630 Fifth Avenue
New York, New York 10020

A portion of this book has appeared in the *Ladies' Home Journal*

First printing

Library of Congress Catalog Card Number: 66-24033
Designed by Edith Fowler
Manufactured in the United States of America
by American Book–Stratford Press, Inc., N.Y.

The author wishes to thank the following companies for permission to reprint material:

Fall River Music, Inc., for permission to use "Where Have All the Flowers Gone?" by Pete Seeger. Copyright © 1961 by Fall River Music, Inc. All rights reserved. Used by permission.

Dolfi Music, Inc., for permission to use "The Lemon Tree" by Will Holt. Copyright © 1961, 1962 by Boulder Music Corp. All rights reserved. Used by permission.

Ludlow Music, Inc., for permission to use "If I Had a Hammer" (The Hammer Song), words and music by Lee Hays and Pete Seeger. Copyright © 1958, 1960, 1962 by Ludlow Music, Inc. All rights reserved. Used by permission.

1385497

To my parents,
who saw me through my first teen age,
and to my husband,
who saw me through my second.

1385437

To my parents,
who saw me through my first teen age,
and to my husband,
who saw me through my second.

*I am deeply grateful to those people whose kindnesses made this book possible—those who offered help knowingly and kept my secret, and those who helped without knowing I had a secret to keep. In an effort to protect both groups, I have done my best to disguise all identities, places, and specific dates, none of which do I plan ever to reveal.*

*L.T.*

# 1

I AM a lucky woman. I like my days. I am a journalist by trade and a housewife by inclination. I have a husband named Frank who is too good to me. I have a pseudo-Tudor house in Long Island, New York, which warms my soul. I don't like tumult. I am not given to derring-do. I like to read and putter and talk to myself, and I have gone to unusual lengths to secure the time to do all three. In the quiet of my house, I feel quite blessed.

Nevertheless, one fall morning—precisely one month before my thirty-fourth birthday and two months before my tenth wedding anniversary—I put on a size 9, pink cotton button-down shirt, a size 11 camel-colored wool skirt which didn't reach my kneecaps, a brown wool cardigan size 36, loafers of a sort (size 5½), with Peds (small), and enrolled as a junior in a high school somewhere in the United States.

Why did I do it?

My purpose was as serious as my adventures were bizarre. I went in the hope that I could restore some perspective to the way we have been looking at our burgeoning younger generation. I had exposed myself to a full broadside of material about today's teenagers and come away with a cause which, I felt, could only be served with a dramatic action.

I must admit, or confess, as the case may be, that I thought it would be fun to be a teenager. All my fantasies of magnificent martyrdom—of the self-sacrifice I was planning in going to live among the savages, to walk alone in the enemy camp—made me smile. I am a prime specimen of the American youth cult. I loathe the idea of growing old. I think I am young, anyway, until I see myself and my contemporaries referred to in print as middle-aged housewives. I'll probably be wearing skirts, sweaters, and knee socks when I'm eighty-seven.

Be really young again: have a gang, rush to classes, go to pep rallies, eat crazy, stay up all night, wear jumpers, bite your nails, sit on the floor, be irresponsible, have fun with a single dollar—and report back what it was like. What healthy, red-blooded, American youth cultist could wake up one morning with that idea in her head, as I did, and say no?

But that's an oversimplification. The idea did not spring, full blown, from the top of my head. It evolved. The day the evolution began, I didn't know I had any feelings about teenagers. I didn't know I cared.

The time was early August. The place, the office of the editor of a monthly magazine. I had just finished an article assignment for him. Routinely, I had been invited back to discuss article ideas for future issues of his magazine. There were a number of celebrities I wanted to profile (for a time, my specialty), and I had gone prepared to discuss them.

The editor seemed distracted. He tried to look interested in what I had to say, but he didn't succeed. When there was a pause in our meeting, he began to swivel his chair, slowly, twenty degrees right, twenty degrees left.

10

"Tell me," he said, as though he weren't sure he wanted me to, "what do you know about teenagers?"

The question surprised me. "Teenagers?" I repeated. "Why?"

"We're going to do a special issue on them," he said. "We've got several articles assigned, but we could use a few more ideas. It would be a good issue for you to work on if there's a particular angle you think you could handle."

He stopped swiveling and looked at me. I was supposed to say something.

"What have you assigned so far?" I asked.

He opened a manila folder on his desktop and leafed through it.

"Well, we're covering the record industry, fan magazines, hippies, how teenage idols are made, teenage buying power, and eating habits. We've got two people on our staff out interviewing them on current events, and we've got a photographer lining up celebrities with teenage kids for a picture story. Nothing else specific. We need some new angles."

I was thinking that they did indeed. I tried not to show how negatively the whole subject struck me, and refrained from saying "Teenagers have been done to death," which is what I felt. But I had to be honest and tell him I had no ideas. I'd think about teenagers and call him.

I left his office annoyed. The meeting, I thought, as I vainly tried to find a cab, had been a waste of time. I didn't want to write anything about teenagers. What did I know about teenagers? So much was being written about them week in, week out. I had just read a long article about how much and why they are drinking these days. I had just thrown away a Sunday supplement completely devoted to studies of their buying power, wonder-

11

ing as I did so which came first, their buying power or the attention to their buying power.

Newspapers and magazines were filled with facts and figures on the teenage crime rate, marriage rate, divorce rate, rate of narcotics addiction, rates of increase in venereal diseases, illegitimate pregnancies, and abortions. Experts by the dozens were poring over and pondering these statistics as though they were tea leaves in the bottom of a cup, which, properly arranged, would reveal the sins of yesterday and the meaning of tomorrow.

Occasionally, there was even something good said, patronizingly, about teenagers: one was a swimming champion, maybe, or two saved a child's life. All old journalistic chestnuts. What could be new about teenagers?

I didn't go straight home. I went to the small library near my favorite supermarket to look for an inspiration. What I found was a number of big numbers: America contains 25,000,000 children between the ages of thirteen and nineteen. That teenage population had increased in the last five years by 24 per cent, the total population by only 8 per cent. For the first time in history, more than half the population of the entire world was under twenty-five. In September, nearly 13,000,000 boys and girls would enroll in the United States high schools—the largest high school enrollment in history. Teenagers' much-publicized "annual discretionary buying power" was variously estimated to be between 10 and 15 billion dollars. Four out of every ten high school boys reportedly had charge accounts, as did two out of every nine high school girls. About 500,000 of each had year-round jobs; 7,000,000 had driving licenses. They owned nearly 400 million dollars' worth of phonograph records and nearly 500 million dollars' worth of cosmetics and toilet goods.

The numbers were mind-boggling. However, they were

meaningless to me in terms of the teenagers I knew casually—cousins, children of my friends, youngsters I had interviewed for articles in the past—and a teenager I knew well: me, seventeen years, an entire teenage, ago.

Numbers had nothing to do with how I looked in my angora socks and loafers, my formals, my blue jeans. Numbers had nothing to do with my gang of girl friends; we were eight blood sisters totally dependent on each other. Numbers had nothing to do with my addiction to the telephone, my staying out too late, being too much in love, sneaking booze, dancing outrageous dances (usually with other girls because the boys didn't know how), listening to records (I must have owned a thousand 78-RPM's and they were something to store, I'll tell you), spending Daddy's money as though it filled a bottomless pit. Particularly did numbers have nothing to do with the ephemeral, exasperating teenage temperament I had in common with every teenage girl I ever knew.

When I got home, I spent the evening swapping stories with my husband about what it had been like to be a teenager. We grew up in very different environments—he on a crowded city block, I on a spacious small-town corner. We grew up in different years—he entered the Army as I entered high school. Yet we had the same kinds of memories. He laughed, nostalgically, about zoot suits and duck's-ass haircuts and long key chains, and giving girls rides on bicycle handles. I laughed, remembering trying to get into cardigans that had to be buttoned down the back, laughed at the number of photographs I used to carry in a wallet, laughed at going to cemeteries to neck because the cops never looked for you there. We both gave wistful salutes to the days when we were giddily happy, illogically sad, arrogantly certain and painfully afraid, all at once.

First thing in the morning I called the magazine editor

to tell him about the article I wanted to write. It would declare that children today are essentially the same as they were in my youth. It would declare that we Americans are responding to the population explosion as though it were an epidemic of a dangerous disease. I was convinced, I told him, that the statistics, the forebodings, the viewing with alarm of teenage behavior, amounted to, at the least, an overstatement of a problem, and at the most, a panicky maligning of the American teenager. "We have lost our perspective," I said. "We have forgotten what it was like to be young."

There was a moment of silence on the phone. Then he spoke: "That's an interesting idea, but it's not true. You could never make a case for yourself."

I said I thought I could. He said I couldn't. He was the editor. He told me to do some more thinking and call him again. "Don't spend too much time on the teenage thing," he suggested. "Get some other, general ideas. I've got to have the teenage issue completely assigned this week."

I went back to the library and read dozens of magazine articles about teenagers which I had missed or chosen to ignore. I crammed books, fiction and nonfiction, purported to be studies of today's youth. I paid attention, for a change, to my friends' worries, complaints, and anecdotes about their teenage children. I prompted discussions with everyone I met socially about what it had been like to be a teenager a teenage ago.

I found little support for my own theory. The consensus was "Kids today are different"; the major difference was in their emotional responses. The parents I talked to, and the educators, sociologists and psychologists I read, were nearly united in their feeling that, unlike yesterday's jiving, ambitious children, today's teenagers are appallingly apathetic. Repeatedly I heard and read, "They are not interested in anything. Nothing moves them. Nothing

14

surprises them. They are passive, emotionless, indifferent."

One parent I spoke to, whose profession is psychiatry, summed up this attitude with terrible bitterness. "Do you find teenagers cynical?" I asked him. "*Cynical?*" he snarled. "Hell, no. In order to be cynical you have to care about something. I wish they *were* cynical."

A devastating analysis. In the extreme, it conjures a vision of an entire generation walking zombielike from crib to grave, living and dying without joy and without protest. I could not accept such an image. For one thing, the same statistics and analyses that were both substantiating and causing such concern about teenagers seemed to me to contradict their ultimate point of view. If, indeed, today's teenagers did not care about anything, why were they drinking too much, marrying and divorcing so hastily, turning on their parents, becoming delinquent, and so on? Even looking at the lighter news was perplexing. It didn't make sense that a generation in hysterics over the Beatles could be dead on its feet. Caring about the frug, in my opinion, was some kind of caring. Again, I tried to look back. I tried to recall what I cared about when I was sweet sixteen. Friends. Teachers. Tests. Clothes. Shiny hair. I didn't remember what else. That doctor who deplored the lack of cynicism among the young—what did he care about twenty or twenty-five years ago? The case for today's "different" teenager was no stronger, I believed, than my own conviction that today's children are children like any others. The truth, I thought, undoubtedly lay between both generalities, buried under several layers of molten words.

I didn't call the magazine editor. I had nothing to offer him except nagging curiosity. He wanted to know about teenagers and so did I. He thought doing a special issue on them would be enlightening; I did not. There was nothing more to do. The only thing missing from my research was "in-depth" interviews with teenagers themselves, a device I considered a waste of time. From previous experience, I knew that teenagers are very wise with reporters. They know, from reading their own press notices, exactly what reporters expect to hear, so that's what they say. They can make it from one end of an interview to the other on pure affectation. In fact, television has turned them into very skilled interviewers themselves. I've often watched school reporters interview celebrities for their newspapers. They're a warmly funny sight. They use a technique that is part cross-examination and part interview, and assume a posture that combines the best of Perry Mason, David Brinkley, and Tom Sawyer.

I had run out of sources. It was time to give up the subject. Time to forget it. Time to store it away and hope that someday . . .

The blinding flash came just like that, in a blinding bonafide, comic-strip, blinking-100-watt-lightbulb flash. At 5 A.M. one August morning I bolted up in bed mouthing cartoon phrases like Eureka! and Holy Cow! and I've Got It! and Why Not? and Of Course! and That's It! and Why Didn't I Think of It Before?

Suppose I could *be* a teenager. Suppose I put on some teenage clothes and wore a wig and mixed in without their knowing I was an adult. If I could *be* a teenager today—even for twenty-four hours . . . if I could communicate with even one teenager on his or her own level . . . of course!

Was it ethical? If precedent was a valid guide, the answer was yes. "Passing" was a time-honored way to get a story. A man had passed for a Negro and written an important book about his experience. A girl had passed for a Playboy Bunny for a now defunct magazine and set the world on fire. Newspaper reporters had

16

passed for inmates of jails and sanatoriums, hospital patients and unwed mothers. Their ends always justified their means.

Had anyone ever tried to pass for a child? I didn't know of anyone except Ginger Rogers in a movie called *The Major and the Minor,* and that didn't count. I had a chance to do something no one had ever done: come of age twice. I was so excited I could hardly breathe.

That, as specifically as possible, was how the idea evolved. Chances are it would never have gone beyond my frontal lobes if any of the four or five people to whom I told it had discouraged me. Surely it would not have grown and spread to such proportions that it swallowed me whole.

If my husband had said, say, "Are you kidding?" I would have dismissed the whole thing as another manifestation of my insomnia problems. If my agent had said, "Do me a favor . . . stay home and write magazine articles like a good girl . . ."

But he didn't and she didn't, so I went to high school. I hadn't the vaguest notion of what I'd find or how I'd respond, but I went.

17

# 2

URBAN HIGH was the biggest school I had ever seen. When it was built in 1926 it was considered a miracle of modern education. "The school of the future," it was called. But it had not aged well. By present standards, it was a graceless, cloistered structure that looked more as if it should be stormed than entered.

The school was probably built originally of stucco-covered frame, but it had been repaired and painted so often that only an expert could be sure. Its most recent color was sand beige.

The classroom buildings went around an entire city block like a great wall. Within the arched and gated entranceways, where you might expect to find either Ticonderoga or the Alamo, there was a huge square courtyard adorned on opposite sides with pairs of stone eagles on pedestals. The buildings were four stories high and contained one row of classrooms on each floor facing the courtyard, another facing the street. Traffic from one building to another passed through connecting passageways on the second and fourth floors.

The school had been built to accommodate 3,000 students, though no one really believed it ever would. The fall I entered it, 4,000 children were expected to register. Such overcrowding was not unique with Urban. The same thing was going on all over the country: 12,700,000 children were entering high school that fall—an increase of 1,000,000 over the year before. Even new schools were filled to capacity and beyond.

Urban, I thought, was the perfect school for my project. It was in a good-sized city west of the Rockies, a city large enough to conceal a transient spy, small enough to be "average," and far enough away from home to give me anonymity and time.

I had wanted very badly to work this project out of my own house so I could have Frank's help and support, but I could not do so. There would have been no way on earth to explain to my neighbors why I was leaving home every day at 8 A.M. and returning at four, wearing flats and carrying school books. I had to go to a city where I knew no one.

At one point in my scheming, I had planned to stay home and enlist the aid of a friend's sixteen-year-old son. When I told her and her husband this, and asked for their help, they responded so strangely that I ruled out involving any teenagers I knew even remotely. They were embarrassed. They behaved as though I had asked if I could seduce their son. "We always wanted Freddy to learn the facts of life from an older woman," they had snickered.

So much for that idea.

The school district in which Urban lay was also ideal. It began on a street of proud-poor row houses, and ended on an affluent residential hill. The sweep of this district offered me the opportunity to observe teenagers of all classes and types in a single environment. It also offered

19

better cover for a transient spy than would a school in a homogeneous neighborhood.

None of these, however, was the reason I happened to be standing outside Urban working up the courage to go in. I was standing in that particular spot on the globe because of Bess.

Bess was the friend I had chosen, from a small list of possibilities, to act as my guardian and sign me into school. I had learned, by calling several school boards, that a guardian with proof of residence was all I needed to register as a transfer student in a high school. Surprisingly, I didn't need either proof of age or school records. The latter would be sent for by my new school, I was told, which was another reason I had to go far from home. The normal, institutional red tape, stretched out over a few thousand miles, I figured, would give me time to get my work done without having to explain why the New York school I was going to claim I attended had never heard of me.

What, precisely, would happen to me if I were "caught" was hard to determine. At least, so said the lawyer I consulted. I might get into trouble for trespassing, he said, or signing a phony name to official records. He seemed much less concerned than I about the possibility of my being hauled before a tribunal. Bess, he thought, might be more seriously embarrassed should the worst happen. She could not be excused as a journalist; I might be. She would have to answer to the community in which she lived; I could go home and melt into the crowd.

I doubt that Bess had any real notion of what she was getting into when she agreed to help me. Though I warned her of the "danger" in our conspiracy, she was too amused by the idea of it to take me seriously. I shall always be in her debt for the positive, unquestioning way she offered me room, board, and her signature next to the word "guardian" on several school documents. The only stipulation she made, when I called her, was that I could not bring any teenagers home from school with me. She didn't want any in the house because, like many people, she felt that teenagers, plural, meant trouble.

Bess was divorced. She had a part-time job which kept her busy during most of the school day. She had a pretty, modest house in a quiet, respectable neighborhood. She knew only a few of her neighbors—and those casually—so it was unlikely that she'd have to explain my presence to more than one or two people. Between us, we made up the story about me which we planned to use for both school officials and her neighbors:

I was born and raised in New York, an only child. My father was a salesman and suddenly he and my mother were divorcing. Papa had disappeared, Mama was somewhere in Nevada and would come for me when the divorce was finalized. Bess was my mother's cousin. She had never seen me before, and she hardly knew my father. If anything went wrong, she was to say I had duped her, too.

I would be the same kind of teenager I had been seventeen years ago: Respectable Middle-class. I would be sixteen, because I could not possibly pass for fifteen, and seventeen was too old.

Coincidentally, the year I was pretending to be born was the year I graduated from high school.

Bess was not particularly keen on my going to the high school in her neighborhood. We had spent my first two days in her town visiting the other two high schools within the city limits, to see if I could go to either of them. I couldn't. There was one high school, a multi-million-dollar marvel just built in one of the rich suburbs, that I could have attended. It was a strictly academic super-school, and in order to get into it as a transfer student, one had to be interviewed by the principal and two other officials. One also had to have an average of at least 85. It would have presented an interesting challenge if I hadn't already been up to my bangs in challenges.

Urban opened for the new school year three days before I had the courage to attempt to storm it. Bess had driven me around it many times, and I had stood on the corners near it, watching kids entering and exiting. I had gone so far as to stick my nose into the courtyard, but I couldn't walk in the door. The morning I decided to hold my nose and jump in, I didn't think I had a 10 per cent chance of passing. As I stood waiting for Bess to park the car and return to escort me, I lowered my estimate another 5 per cent.

It was only 8 A.M.—a most uncivilized hour. In my misty memory of school days, they began at 9, not Urban's 8:20. The air was snappy cold, filled with a serious September smell. I needed the cardigan I carried. I also could have used something warmer than Peds on my feet, but I had been told by a girl back home that "everybody goes bare-legged the first weeks of school to show off their tan," and heaven knows, I wanted to be like everybody.

I wasn't. Nearly all the girls pouring into school had on stockings. A few wore knee socks or anklets with the tops up, but I didn't see any with bare legs.

The two-block radius around Urban was swarming with boys and girls who had walked or driven or bussed to school. There were boys in clean white jeans or dark slacks, or chinos, with shirts and V-necked sweaters, shirts and Perry Como cardigans, shirts and windbreakers. They had crew cuts or longish hair gooed into place. A few had anachronistic pompadours. Those who carried books carried them in one hand, low, against their thighs—a peculiarly masculine posture. The girls who carried books cradled them against their chests.

22

Would I pass in that horde of young girls? Hordes of young girls with teased hair and long, straight hair, and short curly hair. My own hair seemed to be all right. I had had it dyed a shade lighter than my natural dark brown to cover the gray in it. In the hope of hiding my face under hair, I had had it cut blunt below the ears with bangs to my eyebrows. I had given up the idea of a wig as too risky. A wig might get knocked off in a rumble, or displaced in gym class.

"Make me look as young as possible," I had told my hairdresser a week before I left home. "I want to look like a go-go girl. I want a change."

He spent four uninterrupted hours trying to do so. When he finally finished, he stood back and waited for my reaction. I flinched. For three years I had been nurturing my hair to one languid, sophisticated length to support the Merle Oberon image I had of myself. Gone was Merle Oberon, and in her place sat an aging Prince Valiant.

"How old do you think I look?" I asked.

"Twenty-three," said my hairdresser proudly, presenting me a bill for forty dollars.

Immediately following this catastrophe, I met a close friend for a late lunch in the most expensive restaurant in Manhattan. I must have mortified her. She didn't mention my hair, and she didn't look directly at me throughout the entire lunch. Perhaps she thought I'd gone mad. I wonder if she ever went back to that restaurant.

My costume was not bad for my first day of school, but it wasn't perfect. The girls funneling through the gates of Urban wore no obvious "uniform." They had on box-pleated skirts, straight skirts, or full skirts, with clean white blouses or short-sleeved sweaters, and cardigans. A few girls wore dark plaid cotton dresses. September smells of dark plaid cotton.

My own clothes were far too Eastern in style. The

23

difference between Eastern, junior Ivy League clothes and those worn by girls in other parts of the country is subtle but discernible. I would be spotted as an Easterner. My wardrobe was too tailored, too drab in color, for Urban. Urban girls wore more feminine clothes. They wore pink or yellow sweaters; I brought brown and beige. My shirts had button-down collars; theirs had ruffles. My plaid cotton dress was a madras shirtwaist. They wore full-skirted, tightly belted cotton dresses with Peter Pan collars—or ruffles.

I had bought my wardrobe after a shopping trip in the suburbs of New York with a sixteen-year-old cousin. I went with her to browse for her school clothes and, when I left her, retraced our steps and bought everything she had thought was "neat" or "cute." Certainly we had had no trouble finding teenage merchandise. That fall ended a year in which teenage girls had purchased 3.6 billion dollars' worth of clothes; 20 per cent of all clothes sold to the female population, of which teenagers accounted for only 11 per cent. Such facts had spawned blocks of new specialty shops and huge sections of department stores.

Some of the things I tried on grew very mysterious between the time they left the hanger and the time they slipped over my head. One dress in particular had looked awfully cute on the five girls I had seen buying it. It had a royal blue top and a black-and-white-checked bottom, and could be worn either as a jumper or as a sleeveless dress. I put it on just to check size and, oddly, it went straight down to my calves, where it dangled shapelessly. The belt on the hanger was supposed to solve that somehow, but I didn't know how to drape it—under the bust, twice around the waist, three quarters of the way around the hips? When I asked the salesclerk for help she gave me a withering once-over and suggested that perhaps the dress was too young for me. I didn't buy it.

I did buy three skirts, four shirts, two dresses, two cardigans, one fuzzy pullover, one pair of stretch pants, one pair of white jeans, sneakers, a half-slip, a couple of pairs of briefs, two pocketbooks, a stuffable wallet, three headbands, two tiny triangular babushkas like the ones Brigitte Bardot and Jackie Kennedy wear, a pair of loafer-type shoes brand-named Pappagallos, on which I put metal tips and lifts as the kids do, and a trench coat with a zip-out pile lining. I had purchased quite average-priced merchandise and spent approximately $500. My parents had spent no more or less on a comparable wardrobe for me when I was sixteen.

I had been tempted to have my teeth fitted with fake braces but ruled them out in favor of eating and talking. Watching the flow of students into Urban, I was glad I had made such a decision. Very few of them wore braces. This surprised me. I checked later with an orthodontist and learned that by the time children reach high school today they have already been in and out of braces. I wore braces from my fourteenth to my sixteenth years, and, at the time, that was considered young. Most of my friends didn't start wearing them until they were sixteen.

It was bad enough that to become a teenager I had to wear eyeglasses. Fake ones, at that. Normally, I wear glasses to read and to type. At Urban I was wearing them to hide an advanced case of crow's-feet, which my husband calls chicken tracks. Teenagers don't have crow's-feet. Nor do they have the kind of look in their eyes people get from having lived long enough to see more than they care to.

Unfortunately, I was not able to wear my regular glasses because they are framed in heavy, dark (older woman) tortoiseshell. More unfortunately, I didn't have time to get prescription lenses for my new youthful frames, so I was wearing windowpanes. The optometrist

25

had made the phony glasses without question, but he had me come in for a fitting. I found that odd.

If I had really known what I looked like standing there at the gates of Urban, would I have gone on with the game? I don't know. I asked Bess that question one day, and she answered me with another: "If Superman had ever got a good look at himself as Clark Kent," she said, "would he have flown out a window?" It's something to think about.

Other than Bess, only Frank had seen me in my costume. When I had brought all my equipment home, I tested it on him. I put on one whole outfit, from Pappagallos, through glasses, to babushka. What I saw when I looked in the mirror was absolutely fascinating. I'm not sure what you'd call it. It was a mutation of some kind. An apparition. It had a body from one era and a head from another. I had asked Frank to wait in the living room, and as soon as I could tear myself away from my reflection, I wandered slowly down the stairs. When he first saw me, his mouth dropped open for an instant. Otherwise his face was expressionless. Without a word he watched me cross the room. As I reached the couch where he was sitting, he drew back in what looked for all the world like horror.

"My God, get out of here," he said. That's all. To this day I don't know if I looked so freakish I made him feel ill, or so convincing I made him feel old.

Before I left for Bess's, I tried, by staring into a full-length mirror harder than I had in twenty years, to assess, honestly, how old I looked. I couldn't. I have never known how old I looked. People have always thought I looked younger than I am. I believe that is because I am only five feet tall. Normal-sized people think I'm still growing. I weigh between 106 and 112, depending on how much cooking I've been doing. I can—must, in fact—wear junior sizes. Sometimes even "petites" have to be shortened for me.

26

My mother tells me, when I wear Bermuda shorts and a shirt, that I look twelve. She's right in one respect. I am the height of today's average twelve-year-old. The girls who were sweeping past me into the halls of Urban averaged at least three inches taller than I. I was a runty teenager, my second time around.

"Hi," they were calling to each other. "Hi! Come to my locker with me. Hi! See you at lunch." And their voices were pitched an octave higher than my own. Their laughter came from mid-tongue. Their hands were full and plump. Their upper arms were thin and firm. Their stomachs were flat. They had no lines on their faces—none. No diagonal creases between the mouth and nose, no lines under the eyes. From where I stood, I couldn't even find a cheekbone in the hordes of girls.

"Are you ready?" asked Bess, as she came up behind me. If she hadn't given me a small, firm shove, I think I'd still be standing there.

# 3

$T$HE INSIDE of Urban was surprisingly somber. I had expected the corridors to be wide and bright, but they were like subway tunnels. When I first walked into the school, I found myself slouching because I felt that if I straightened up too fast I would hit my head on the ceiling. In reality, the ceiling was at least fifteen feet high.

The floors and baseboards were stained a long-lost brown. The walls were colorless. The heavy doors of the rooms along the halls had been stained dark brown a thousand times. What warmth there might have been in any of the wood—the floors and the doors—was buried under shellac so thick it had become veneer. Forty years of varnish had made the halls of Urban very shiny, but shiny like a thickly polished, dirty old shoe.

The frenzy of motion around me was surprising, too. The halls were alive with kids running or moving at a fast trot. They went in all directions at once, two, three, or four abreast, talking as fast as they moved. I felt no relationship to them at all. I was really too scared, too tight, to see them as people, or to wonder whether they noticed me. Mostly, I just kept my eyes on the floor and waited for whatever was going to happen to happen.

Bess stopped a young man and asked the way to the attendance office. He pointed without turning his head, irritated at having his pace broken. We followed his index finger to a small room split in half by a high counter, behind which were three women, two typewriter desks, and floor-to-ceiling filing cabinets.

Bess walked up to the counter. I found a wooden chair near the wall and sat in it with my head down and my hands clenched in my lap. If I could just keep anyone from seeing my face or my hands, *maybe* I'd make it.

"Can I help you?" asked one of the women.

"Yes, please," said Bess. She leaned in toward the woman and lowered her voice.

"This child has been sent to me to take care of. Her mother's getting a divorce."

The woman glanced at me.

Bess lowered her voice still further. "I'd like to register her in school as soon as possible. She's very upset, you see, and I think if she starts school right away she'll be better off. I don't know what to do with her. You know? Teenagers. You know?"

"Where's her mother?" asked the woman.

"Nevada," Bess said.

"Where's her father?"

Bess whispered, "Nobody knows. It's terrible. He just disappeared. Awful."

The woman nodded, looking at me again—longer, this time. She shook her head. "Awful," she said. "Divorce, divorce, that's all you hear about these days."

"Awful," said Bess.

"Well, don't worry," said the woman. "She won't feel strange in a few days. Half the children in this school have divorced parents. Maybe more."

"Well, may I just sign her in, please? I go to work, you see, and I'm late."

"Oh, well, you're in the wrong office," said the woman. "You'll have to see the Dean of Girls. You and the youngster. Here, you go out this door and turn right. You'll see a sign on the door."

Out in the hall I asked Bess if she'd ever heard of having a Dean of Girls in a high school.

"Shhhh," she said.

The dean was a stereotype. Why do people so often look the part? Is it that certain jobs attract people of certain specific physical characteristics? Or do people begin to look their parts after they've had them for a while? Puzzling. But there was the Dean of Girls: tall, thin, gray-haired, of indeterminable age, taut, and intimidating.

She sat behind a desk in a cubbyhole guarded by a row of assistants. When we walked into her presence, she rose, shook Bess's hand, and nodded to me. Then she sat down, gesturing for us to do the same. She listened politely while Bess told her our much-rehearsed story. Toward the end of the tale, she reached into the top drawer of her desk for a thin sheaf of papers. As soon as Bess stopped talking, the dean picked up a pen. "I see," she said.

"What is the name of the school you last attended?" she asked me.

"South Suburban," I mumbled.

"In New York?" she asked.

I nodded.

"That's a fine school," she said. "What year were you going to start there?"

"Junior," I mumbled.

"We call that low eleven," she said. "What was your average?"

"She was very bright," said Bess.

The dean pursed her mouth and gave Bess a nasty look. "What was your average?" she repeated.

"B-plus," I mumbled.

30

"Can't you look *up,* girl, when you speak?" the dean snapped. "Can't you look me in the eye?"

I looked up quickly and flashed her a grin.

The dean picked up several papers and handed them to Bess. "Would you fill these out, please?" she said.

"Now?" asked Bess.

"Now," said the dean.

Bess began writing. In less than a minute she reached a question she didn't know how to answer. The dean, seeing her hesitate, suggested she fill the papers out with me. We wrote: Father's address, unknown; Mother's address, unknown; Father's occupation, salesman; Mother's, free-lance designer. Age, grade, lies, lies, lies.

When we finished, the dean gave Bess three more papers to fill out and have notarized. ("No rush, but when you can, please.") She apologized for having so little time to give us, and told us how to find the next person we had to see, my guidance counselor.

"We're happy to have you . . . er . . . ah"—she looked at her desktop—"Lyn. We know you'll do just fine here."

As we went out the door, Bess made a dent in my fifth rib with her right elbow.

The guidance counselor was a kindly godmother type, fortyish, round, gentle, soft-spoken, patient, and very much impressed with Bess, who, I forgot to mention, has a most regal air. Her office was filled with students waiting to see her, but she called Bess in ahead of them all. While I sat in the shadows, the two women discussed my case, looking at me from time to time, shaking their heads sympathetically. That done, I was summoned into their circle.

In a voice that assured me the operation wouldn't hurt, my counselor began: "Now then, Lyn dear, we'll make up your schedule. Your guardian tells me you're a very bright girl." She smiled. I dropped my eyes modestly.

"Have you had U.S. 1?" she asked.

31

Unsure of what that was, I shook my head no. She put me down for U.S. 1.

"What is that?" asked Bess.

"American history," said the counselor. "They've changed the names of everything since our day."

"I thought it was a superhighway," jollied Bess.

The counselor laughed. "Aren't you lucky to have such a guardian?" she said to me. "Why, you're going to have such fun out here. You won't miss New York at all. . . . Now then. How about a language? Mrs. . . . umm, Mrs. . . . your guardian tells me you've been taking French."

Mistake number one. I knew no French. I threw Bess a helpless look.

"She's had enough French," Bess said.

"Yes. I don't like French," I mumbled.

"Can't you look at me when you talk?" the lady asked in a kindly voice. I looked up at her. She smiled and patted my hand. I didn't have to take French, she said. What else would I like? German? Russian?

"I'd like to take Spanish. Do you have that?"

"Why, yes," said the lady, looking pleased. "I used to teach it. I *love* the sound of Spanish, don't you? *Muy bien* . . . *Muy bien* . . . Such a shame you weren't here last year. You could have been in my class." She wrote me into Spanish 1.

"Do you think she should take geometry this semester?" she asked Bess. Bess shook her head no.

"I don't either," said the counselor. "Too much else to do." She smiled at me. "We'll go easy on you until you get used to us."

She thought I could handle American literature, the course in English for juniors, and I had to take G.P.E. (General Physical Education) five days a week. (Five days a week?) I could have study hall, which they thought would be relaxing, and one other elective.

32

I didn't remember having electives in high school. I didn't know what to elect. I sat there like a zombie, trying to think of something. That's how I got scheduled for public speaking to help me get over my shyness.

"Now for home room . . . let's see. I think you'd like Mrs. Brown. Yes. Mrs. Brown. There. Well. That wasn't so bad, was it?"

I looked at Bess. She smiled. I smiled. My counselor stood up. Our meeting was over. She didn't ask me whether I wanted to go to college, or where; she didn't ask me what I wanted to be when I grew up. In less time than it would take me to retype this chapter, I had become a low eleven in Urban High School.

# 4

My FIRST CLASS was history, and the schedule I was carrying said that it was in Room 429. Obviously, I had to get to the fourth floor, but of which wing, by which staircase?

I had not expected to find myself adrift in the halls of Urban without friend, foe, compass or paddle. Whenever I had pictured my first day of school I had imagined I would be assigned a girl guide who would lead me to my classes, introduce me to teachers and pals, and generally see to my immediate assimilation. That was the way new students were handled in my day, and still are in many schools, but perhaps such a system would have been impossible at Urban. There were four hundred transfer students registered by the time I signed in, and more coming every day. Certainly it would have been difficult to give personal attention to each one. On the other hand, the size of the school made it imperative that new students be assisted so they wouldn't feel thoroughly lost, as I did.

Bess had fled. My guidance counselor had set me loose with the assurance that I could call on her if I needed anything at all. Students and teachers were behind closed doors having "home room." I was totally alone, and totally bewildered.

Suddenly a bell clanged, signaling the end of home room and the beginning of the serious day. All the doors along the hall sprang open simultaneously. Through them shot a few thousand students, determined to make the next ten minutes of their lives really count. I had the distinct impression they were all running toward me, indeed might run right over me if I didn't make a quick move. As it turned out, they had good reason to stream in my direction; I happened to be standing in front of a staircase, hidden for the moment by swinging doors. Once the students started for the stairs, the doors were in steady motion, swinging wickedly open and wickedly back. No one made the slightest effort to keep the doors from flattening a body on the back swing.

The stairway presented another obstacle course. On it were two lanes of traffic going up, two lanes coming down, half of each breaking out of line at the bottom of the steps to go into a hall, and a whole new crowd breaking in to get to the next floor. It was possible to move in the two outside lanes with relative safety if you stayed flat against the wall. In the two center lanes, danger loomed on every riser. Students passing there bashed into each other and their protruding books bruised any limb that happened to get in the way.

It is probably needless to say that I was late getting to Room 429. The room was filled when I got there. There were a number of students in front of the teacher's desk, waiting to be signed in, and I joined them.

The teacher's name was Mr. Goodman. He was about five feet six, was just one side or the other of forty, wore glasses and lightweight tweeds, and had a round, pleasant face. When I finally got to him, to get his signature on my schedule, he was wearing a very pained expression. He looked at my program, sighed, and handed it back to me. "I have no more room in this class," he said.

I didn't know how I was supposed to respond to this news, so I just stood there. He sighed again, sat down behind his desk, scribbled something on a scrap of paper, folded it, and placed it in my hand, saying, "Take this to your counselor." The note read: "If you want me to go over the limit of thirty-six for this girl, please sign this."

My counselor was not in the room where I had met her. She was in the gym supervising programming. I was amazed that there was still so much turmoil taking place over schedules. There were at least two hundred kids in that gym, lowing and braying and bellowing. An adult was trying to get them to form lines but they wouldn't. They had come to make changes. They declared their complaints to anyone else who would listen. A few even talked to me.

"Christ, I'm stuck with Jones-head for history. Christ, he gives a test every day. I'm gonna get Smith for history, boy. I'm not gonna stay in that shit-class."

"I've *got* to take Spanish. I don't care. Ardith and Eloise both have Spanish and we always do our homework together. You know. And if they have Spanish this term and I don't have it till next term, you *know*. Golly, I've *got* to get Spanish."

"I *can't* take geometry now. I *can't*. I've got my guitar lessons four times a week and when am I supposed to *practice?*"

"I've got to have first lunch period. I've got low blood pressure. My mother won't let me take second lunch period. I'll get my doctor to call. I *can't* eat that late; I'll faint."

"My doctor *gave* me a note about my arthritis. I told her that. I can't take gym. They've got to let me out of it. I don't care. I just won't go. They can kick me out of school."

"Christ. I got Jugger-head for lit. That shit really has it in for me. He'll flunk me if I sneeze. I gotta switch. I'll tell 'em something. I'll think of something."

Behind a rope that separated the students from the teachers tending them was my counselor. She was in the middle of the biggest, most protesting crowd, fending off complaints, ignoring the worst troublemakers, and juggling an occasional schedule. She looked unreachable; I gave up hope of getting to her for a few hours. I turned away from her and looked for a line to get into, or someplace safe to stand. Then I heard her call my name. The sound of it in that place where I knew no one startled me.

"Lyn," she shouted over the din, "are you having trouble already?" She gestured me forward. I reached through a crowd and gave her Mr. Goodman's note, which she read with a smile. She leaned against the wall, wrote an answer on the back of the note, and returned it to me. She also gave me a slip of paper explaining why I was at liberty during class time. On the way back up to the fourth floor, I read what she had written. It was: "Yes, *please*. I promise I won't ask again."

By the time I got to the door of history class, the bell rang ending the period. I flattened myself against the wall until the room emptied, and then handed the note to Mr. Goodman, who signed me into his class with one comment: "You have a powerful friend here." A powerful friend—i.e., somebody to keep an eye on me—was not exactly what I needed. My counselor worried me the rest of the day, but I shouldn't have given her a thought. When I saw her twenty-four hours later, she didn't know me.

Study hall was in the basement, one flight below the

37

ground floor. I was late getting there. There were only about a dozen in the class, scattered over the large room I later learned was part of the cafeteria. The room had a low ceiling, pale green walls in need of painting, and long bare wooden tables every few feet. Seated at one table were three boys in light jeans, white shirts, and sneakers. Each had dark hair cut short; from the back they looked like triplets. At another table was a pair of girls sitting very close and giggling. One had light hair teased into a variety of French roll and was not bad-looking. The other was a humdinger, as they used to say in the Ice Age. She had thick black hair—dyed, I think—worn in a short pageboy and draped over one eye, thin black eyebrows, pale skin, shadows under her eyes, and a beauty mark near her left nostril. She had on a neon-blue sweater and a very knowing look. I dubbed her Liz.

I chose a stool next to a girl who looked as if she would make an interesting friend. She was blond, willowy, big-eyed, dressed out of *Seventeen,* and wore braces. She would have been a perfect doll except that her skin was badly broken out. When I sat down, she turned away from me and opened a paperbound copy of *Lord of the Flies.* I tapped her on the shoulder and asked her if we were allowed to talk in study hall. She shrugged.

An undersized boy two seats to my left asked me how to spell "wander." I didn't know if I should know, but I told him. He had a paperbound copy of *Lord of the Flies* on top of his books.

Diagonally across the room, a Negro boy in a red shirt sat alone, hunched over his books. Sometimes he would rest his head on his arms. He was big, muscular, and handsome. A pair of fruit boots protruded from behind a pole near him. I couldn't see what they belonged to. They just protruded, like a stage prop, reminding me that this wasn't the forties, wasn't my own high school study hall. Fruit boots hadn't existed in the forties.

The teacher sat with his back to the room, which seemed to me to be pretty brave of him. Nothing untoward happened, however—no spitballs thrown, no shivs unsheathed, no pot distributed; no one raped anyone. Except for the two girls who knew each other, and they talked steadily, everyone was quietly hunched over some book or other.

I decided to give the girl next to me another try. I groped in my purse for a street map and a pack of gum, figuring the girl would say to herself "What ho, a stranger in our midst" and ask me if she could have some gum. Wrong again. She arched her back and went on reading. She didn't even mention that it was against the rules to chew gum. I found that out later, the hard way.

I was beginning to be terribly worried about ever making friends with any of my classmates, but tried not to brood about it. For distraction, I opened my notebook and started a letter to my husband, whose fortieth birthday it was that day and whom I missed desperately.

Dear Frank. He had been so wonderful about getting me ready to leave home. Only once did he show any of the anxiety he has since admitted he felt about the madness that had taken over our household the week before I left. It was at seven one morning. He was standing near his sock drawer, looking for a black pair among the navy ones. Suddenly he flipped the drawer shut and turned to me.

"Are you going to let them paw you?" he demanded.

"Are I going to let who paw me?" I inquired from bed.

"Teenage boys."

"How come you never asked me if I was going to let any of the few hundred men I've interviewed paw me?" I asked.

"Because none of them was a teenage boy," he answered.

I laughed. He didn't. Somehow, I'd never thought

about the possibility of a teenage boy pawing me. It seemed a most unlikely problem at the time Frank mentioned it, and even more unlikely once I got a look at me in my disguise. I couldn't imagine any of the boys in study hall trying to paw me. Maybe there'd be someone in my English class. Anyway, it was a situation I simply couldn't anticipate. I'd have to figure out what to do about it when and if it happened.

Frank and I had barely even said goodbye. We were both terribly self-conscious at the airport; when he took me to the plane, it was the first time we had been in public together with me in my kiddy clothes. What did we look like as a pair? Father and daughter? Sister and brother? Humbert Humbert and Lolita? There was no way to know, so we just played it cool. We didn't talk and we didn't kiss goodbye.

My dearest husband,

*I write you from study hall. I've no homework to do yet so I'll sneak the time now rather than try to write you in the evening*

The bell signaling the end of second period aborted my letter and scared the stuff out of me. Once I got used to the bell I began to anticipate it as everyone else did, but that first morning every time it rang I felt as if the sound was trapped in the hollow of my bones.

My third class, Spanish, was on the third floor in the next building, Room 303. I ran all the way, wishing I hadn't put metal tips on my shoes; they destroyed my traction. There was a dreadful racket on the third floor, and as I walked toward 303 it grew louder. Room 303 was where the noise was originating.

Running up the last aisle of the room were two boys, one pursuing the other. As they ran, they pushed aside

some desks and jumped over others. Four boys, one standing, three sitting, were shouting encouragement to the one
in the lead.

"Over here, Tony," the standee said with a laugh. Then
he jumped up on his chair and waved his arms.

In the front of the room stood a distraught-looking
young lady who, from the tone of her voice, had to be the
teacher. "*Sit down, all of you!*" she cried. The chase went
on. She screamed, "SIT DOWN, I SAID!"

Tony careened into a desk, making sound effects like
a crashing jet. The other racer leap-frogged over a desk
and, likewise, crash-landed.

"Now listen, you boys!" the teacher shouted. "I'm not
going to put up with this one more minute. If you don't
start shaping up, you can just ship out of here."

Laughter.

"I'm not kidding. Now stop it."

"Hey, Tony. Teach said shut up," said one of the boys.

The teacher, Miss Zorri, turned to close the door. Tony
threw a pencil at his former pursuer. They laughed. Then,
for a moment, the room grew quiet. There were sixteen
pupils in it: the six rowdies and four other boys, plus six
girls, two of whom were quite pretty. The rowdies were
surprisingly nice-looking boys, a couple of them afflicted
slightly with acne, but all well-groomed and well-
dressed. One of them, called Mickey by his friends, was a
particularly good-looking boy, tall, with thick dark blond
wavy hair and light eyes. He wore finely creased slacks
with a white shirt and black V-necked sweater—a nattier
outfit by far than any I'd seen on his classmates. I figured
he might be one of the affluent delinquents I'd read about,
and decided to keep an eye on him.

Miss Zorri was astonishingly young-looking. She must
have been right out of college. She was pretty and shapely
but in need of a do-over by the beauty department of

41

*Glamour.* I could picture the dramatic moment when a chic, lithe, hip young beauty editor, her 184 I.Q. in full flower, her backless Cordovan oxfords planted firmly on the ground, her welt-seamed little jersey dress allowing her full freedom of movement, wrenched the pin from the back of Miss Zorri's upsweep and let her black hair fall to the small of her back, stomped on Miss Zorri's gray-rimmed eyeglasses and straightened the eyebrows thus revealed, and committed her, wrapped in swaddling, to the House of Revlon.

Alas, *Glamour* was light-years away, Miss Zorri but five feet from my desk, toying with her hair. She kept finding wisps of it on the back of her neck, which she tried to tuck back into their French roll. She tugged at her skirt and yanked at the bottom of her sweater in a kind of four-four rhythm. Whenever she saw one of the rowdies looking at her, she averted her eyes and blushed.

Class was divided into two groups: those who had taken Spanish before and were enrolled in Spanish 2, and those who had not. The rowdies were among the half taking Spanish 2. It fell to Miss Zorri to find a way to teach both halves simultaneously.

The first thing she did was physically separate the two groups.

"Spanish Ones, will you please sit in the first two rows?" she asked firmly. "Spanish Twos, take rows three and four."

We Ones got up obediently and took our proper seats. The Twos stayed right where they were and stared aggressively at Teacher. She stared back, giggled, shrugged, and walked over to our section to teach us to say "Good morning. How are you?"

"*Buenos Días. ¿Cómo está usted?*"

"I thought that meant good night," said Tony, in a stage whisper.

"It does," said Mickey. "Teach doesn't know when it's night."

"Repeat after me" said Teacher to the Ones, "*Buenos días.*"

"BUENOS DÍAS," shouted the rowdies, in unison.

Miss Zorri stamped her foot. "Now I'm talking to the Ones, and you Twos over there keep quiet."

From row four came a muffled hoot. Everybody laughed. Two more hoots.

Miss Zorri laughed. "Now come on," she said.

"Now come on," mimicked Tony in falsetto.

"Come ON," said Mickey, stamping his foot.

The class dissolved into laughter and conversation. I wondered what Miss Zorri's next move would possibly be, and she no doubt was wondering too, when she was blissfully saved by a piercingly urgent bell. Though I hadn't heard that particular sound in seventeen years, I knew exactly what it was and responded accordingly: fire drill. Time to spring to your feet. Time to drop everything and get some air. Time to look for your boyfriend or pass notes and find out the answer to test questions.

We all filed out the door, Miss Zorri barking instructions behind us: "Go to the rear hall. Don't run. Mickey, fix the windows. Everybody stay in line. Don't run. *Don't run!* DON'T RUN, I SAID!"

In just three minutes the entire population of Urban was standing in the city street. So many of them. So *many.*

Two boys behind me were discussing a girl out of my range of vision:

First Boy: Just look at that Judy Brown. She bugs the *shit* out of me. She really *bugs* me. Just look at her.

Second Boy: Yeah.

First Boy: I just want to get a flamethrower and go whoosh right through that.

(Did he love her, hate her, covet her?)

Second Boy: Yeah.

First Boy: *Look* at her. How does she get those rats in her hair? Boy. Look at that. (He stood on tiptoes.) She's talking to O'Brien. There's a pair. What a pig.

Second Boy: Does she?

First Boy: If *she* doesn't, it's not by choice; nobody would touch her. Boy, look at her. God, she's horrible.

Second Boy: Makes me wanna barf.

All the way back into the building they strained and watched. I never did see the girl under surveillance. The boys were scrawny, unwashed, and had acne.

Back in Spanish class Miss Zorri's problems took up where they had left off. Mickey seemed pathologically incapable of keeping quiet. And every time he opened his mouth he set off his friends. Punk and firecrackers. They mimicked the teacher, told jokes, and answered questions she asked other students—all out loud.

Miss Zorri responded with threats: "I'm going to start calling you names," she said. (?) "How would you like to be late for your fourth period?" she asked, followed by "What floor is this?" A voice thrust, "Fourth." She parried, "Do you suppose somebody would crack their skull if I threw them out of the window?" (Which was not only impossible but also ungrammatical.)

She threatened to flunk anyone who pronounced an "h" in a Spanish word, and she threatened to make the rowdies sit in the front row. The latter threat she finally carried out over a chorus of grumbling and shuffling.

Between threats she conjugated "to be" and "to have" on the blackboard for the Ones. As the period drew to a close, Mickey and Tony were softly singing "La Paloma" while everyone else choked on giggles. Miss Zorri gave me a Spanish textbook, my first, saying, "Look this over by tomorrow." She told the rest of the class to keep reading the text.

44

Clearly, Spanish class was going to be an adventure for us all.

Next came English class, one wing over and to the right. I got lost. By the time I got signed into the class, there was only one vacant desk, right under the teacher's nose. I had no choice but to settle into it.

The English teacher, Mr. Fells, was a meek-looking man of average height. He was pale, slim, and probably in his late thirties. He quieted the class quickly and announced he woud resume reading aloud where he'd left off the previous period: in the middle of a Shirley Jackson short story called "The Lottery." He stepped to the front of his desk, cleared his throat, flipped through the pages of a paperbound book, and began to read:

"Just as Mr. Summers finally left off talking and turned to the assembled villagers, Mrs. Hutchinson came hurriedly along the path to the square, her sweater thrown over her shoulders, and slid into place in the back of the crowd. 'Clean forgot what day it was,' she said to Mrs. Delacroix, who stood next to her, and they both laughed softly. . . ."

Slowly and dramatically Mr. Fells paced back and forth in front of his desk, gesturing and grimacing, changing the pitch of his voice for each new character. Slowly and dramatically he worked at making the chilling story come alive. There was only one flaw in his performance: The zipper on his fly was not locked, and as he paced, it was inching open.

Absurd.

It is absurd, anyway, to find yourself sitting at a school desk again, trying to find a comfortable spot to lean on, trying to pay attention, trying to stay awake, trying to stretch your legs without ramming the boy too big for the desk in front of you. The desks at Urban were just like

45

standard ones of my own day. In fact, everything about Urban was beginning to look strangely familiar. The blackboard with chalk dust in the troughs, the green metal wastebaskets, the parchment window shades, the long hooked poles used to open the windows. And yes, the students slouching in their chairs, or leaning forward, chin in palm. I had seen these kids before. I had been here before. I had even been taught by this teacher—not English, but history. Tenth-grade history. He was my tenth-grade history teacher, by God, I'd swear to it.

He was nearing the end of "The Lottery":

". . . Old Man Warner was saying, 'Come on, come on, everyone.' Steve Adams was in the front of the crowd of villagers, with Mrs. Graves beside him.

" 'It isn't fair, it isn't right,' Mrs. Hutchinson screamed, and then they were upon her."

He finished reading. He closed the book the way a man of God would close the Bible, and set it down reverently on his desk behind him. He removed his glasses, wiped them carefully, put them back on, and looked, with great deliberation, at the class, one row at a time. He cleared his throat.

"Every June someone in the village got stoned to death," he said. "Now. Shirley Jackson was trying to make a comment about people. What was it?"

The class shifted self-consciously. A few students began leafing through their notebooks. No one raised a hand to answer his question. All looked down at their desktops.

"Can you see any parallel events in life today?" he asked.

There was another self-conscious pause. Then a boy raised his hand and said "Lee Oswald."

"What about Lee Oswald?" the teacher asked.

"Well, it's like killing Lee Oswald," the boy mumbled.

The teacher made no comment. He asked for other parallels. When no one volunteered any, he continued.

"We love to see somebody else get it," he said. Then he talked about how rotten people are by nature and how cruel the world is, and asked, "Why do you venture outside every morning?"

No one answered.

What did the thirty-five young people in that room think? I wondered. Were they listening? Were they interested? Did they notice that the teacher's fly was now fully unzipped? Yes, that they noticed. You could tell from the way they were poking each other and snickering.

There were so many distractions. How did they concentrate? Now there was a roaring crowd outside in the courtyard. The windows were open to let in the noonday sun, and the sounds of first lunch hour filled the air. I was scheduled for second shift and I was starved. Were they? The morning seemed so long. The chair was so uncomfortable.

I marveled at my classmates. How did they manage to pay attention?

The girl next to me had a paperbound copy of *Lord of the Flies* on top of her books. So did the boy next to her.

Across the room a girl with yé-yé hair and crazy eyeglasses leaned over to pick her purse off the floor, cautiously unsnapped it, and took from it a small compact, which she propped open on her notebook. Then she slid a comb out of the bag, and, squinting studiously at herself, she combed her nice neat bangs flat down her forehead, once, twice . . . again, again, again. As though it were some kind of signal, all of a sudden every girl in the room was reaching for a comb or small hairbrush, powder, mascara, and lip pomade (lipstick was out that September). Then the boys began—not all of them; say ten, or twelve. They reached surreptitiously into shirt pockets or back pants pockets, and palmed small combs through their sidelocks. It had to be some kind of ritual.

I reached for my comb, too, but my timing was off. By

the time I assembled my equipment the lunch bell
sounded, setting off a human stampede the like of which
has not been recorded since the Cimarron land rush.
When the dust settled, I returned compact and comb to
the tweed pocketbook I had purchased for six dollars in
the teenage department of Saks and gave the pack of
Kents hidden in the bottom of it a loving pinch. I would
gladly have traded my entire kingdom for one deep inhale
and the directions to the nearest john.

# 5

Even before the lunch bell had stopped ringing, everyone was gone, except one little mouse of a girl who looked at me and smiled forlornly.

"Hi," she said. "I saw you making up your schedule this morning. I'm new here, too. Are you eating with anyone?"

"Unh-unh," I said. "You?"

"Unh-unh," she replied. "Do you want to eat together?" I nodded and told her I didn't know where the cafeteria was. "I was there for a class this morning, but I don't think I could find it again."

"There aren't any classes in the cafeteria," she said.

I shrugged.

"Well anyway," she said, "I know where it is. Let's go. My name's Glenda. What's yours?"

The stairway, normally jammed, was nearly deserted.

"I guess we're late," Glenda observed. We started down. "In my school," she said slowly, "when there was a new student somebody was assigned to take care of her."

"Mine, too," I said.

Silence. Landing, right turn, descent.

"We wouldn't expect anybody to find her way around alone and not meet anybody," said Glenda.

"We wouldn't either," said I.

Step, step, step, step. Right turn.

"Gosh, where *is* the cafeteria?" I inquired.

"Down a ways. Under the floor where the gym is." Five boys banged through the swinging doors on the landing and ran ahead of us, taking two steps at a time. Glenda recoiled, then straightened.

"Where are you from?" she asked me.

"Where are *you* from?"

"How do you like it here?"

"How do *you* like it here?"

"What grade are you in?"

"What grade are *you* in?"

"What courses are you taking?"

"What courses are *you* taking?"

At the bottom of the steps we hesitated, staring at the restive mob that filled the corridor in front of the cafeteria.

Glenda looked at me and shrugged. "Do you have a locker?" she asked. I didn't. "Neither do I," she said. "We'll have to carry all our stuff in with us. Well, come on."

Momentum carried us through the mob to a line at the door which forked and became two lines, one for hot food, one for cold. Glenda hopped on the hot line (so to speak), and I followed, picking up a tray, plate, spoon and fork on the way. There were no knives. When Glenda held out her plate, I held out mine. Food was dropped on it by a lady in a freshly starched, freshly ironed, and freshly soiled white uniform.

There were several desserts, but I couldn't make up my mind fast enough and got shoved straight past them to the checkout girl. "How much do I owe you?" I asked.

"Thirty-five cents," said the checkout girl. "Whadja think it was, a dollar?" The boy behind me laughed. She

50

flipped the change on my tray and I caught up with Glenda, who was looking for a place to sit.

Every table was filled to overflowing with students, food and paraphernalia. We stood and stood, balancing trays, books, and sweaters. Finally Glenda spotted an empty table corner and took a step. We tried to push through what should have been corridors between the tables.

"Excuse me. Excuse me, please. Excuse me," she said. Nobody moved.

When we reached the space Glenda had seen, we found it heaped with books. Glenda tapped the girl nearest them on the shoulder. "Excuse me," she said. The girl flipped out one arm and covered the books. "These seats are taken," she said. We moved away.

Two more times we tried to sit down and were told the places were reserved. By the time we found two vacant stools and settled at the end of a table, everyone around us had finished eating and cleared out. We opened our milk cartons, shot the papers off our straws and started lunch.

On my plate there was a ball of mashed potatoes with meat sauce poured over it. Next to that was canned corn, and tilted against the edge of the plate was a roll with a pat of butter. Glenda had the same plus a bowl filled with small cubes of Jello.

Just as we mushed our potatoes and took the first bite, a man in fatigues came by blowing a whistle. When he stopped blowing he bellowed, "All right, everybody, hurry it up. You got a lot to do in here yet. Let's get movin' . . . let's get movin'."

"When's lunch hour over?" I asked Glenda.

She shrugged.

"I guess we'd better go or the warden will get us," I said.

51

She giggled. "Warden. That's funny. He's the monitor. Didn't you have one of those in your school?" I shook my head no.

The whistle blew again, this time directly over our shoulders. We both shrugged, stood up, collected our books, and headed for the exit. We took two giant steps and there was the warden, arms akimbo.

"Where you going, girls?" he asked.

"Outside," said Glenda in a wee voice.

"Oh, no you're not," he said. "You're gonna clean up your mess just like everybody else."

We looked where he was pointing, shrugged, backed up, picked up our trays, dumped the milk cartons in the milk carton basket, dumped the food into a garbage can, deposited the dishes on a pile of dirty dishes, tossed the silverware on a pile of dirty silverware, placed the trays where we'd picked them up originally, returned to the table for books and things, and went outside.

Directly beyond the door was a group of girls with bizarre, teased hairdos. They wore tight sweaters or sheer blouses with dark, tight skirts. Surrounding them were boys with longish stringy hair wearing tight black pants and dark zippered jackets.

"They look bad news," whispered Glenda.

I nodded.

Beyond them were thousands of kids clustered in the huge courtyard. They were shifting their feet, moving their arms, and making a hum like a turnpike on a summer Sunday.

Glenda and I sat down on a low stone wall, back to back.

"I wonder why that man told us to leave," she said. "There's lots of time. We could have finished our lunch."

"Do you know where the john is?" I asked her.

"Unh-unh," she said. "Anyway, you can't go in the building till the bell rings."

We changed position, swinging our feet off the wall and turning so we could see the kids as they came out the cafeteria doors.

"In my old school we weren't allowed to wear our hair like that," she said, gesturing discreetly toward the tough-looking group. "Look at that one! Look at *that* one! We weren't allowed to wear our skirts so short, and we couldn't wear stockings to school. We had to wear these." She lifted her foot so I could see her saddle shoes and anklets.

I nodded.

"There's some nice girls over there," she said, pointing. "I wonder if they're in low eleven." Then she shook her head despairingly. "I'm so out of place here," she sighed. "So out of place."

Poor Glenda. I knew just how she felt.

# 6

A TANNED, stocky, blond low eleven in a plaid skirt and navy blazer was standing at the foot of the auditorium stage waving her hands at her audience. "Let's everybody get quiet," she shouted. "Okay, quiet. Listen, everybody move up here and fill the front rows. Okay? Everybody just move up here except anyone new. Anyone new should come up on the stage and sign in. And listen, everybody please keep quiet until everybody's signed in. If you signed in this morning, you don't have to sign in again even if you switched classes. Or do you?"

The girl turned to a woman sitting at a table behind her. "Miss Jeffries, if you signed in this morning and then changed classes and now you're in this class, do you have to sign in again?" Miss Jeffries nodded. "Yes, you do have to," said the girl. "You do have to, if you changed to this class even if you signed in this morning, sign in again for this class.

"Hi, Jen," she said to somebody in the front row. "Did you switch to here? Where's Elk?" She scanned the auditorium. "Oh, hi, Elk," she waved.

"So okay. Everybody who has to sign in has to sign in.

Any questions?" There were none. The girl strode to a spot behind Miss Jeffries' left shoulder and stood at attention.

This was gym class, the teenage girl's anathema. Also, I suspected, anathema to any girl pretending to be a teenager. I had put off thinking about this particular fifty minutes all morning because I couldn't imagine any way to get through it successfully. An athletic washout, I was always the type that got excessive attention from gym teachers, either because I annoyed them or because they saw in me a magnificent challenge. From the moment I began to think seriously about what would be involved in going back to school, I had planned to deal with the realities of gym class—the scrutiny by teachers, the locker room, the group shower, the new physical-fitness-for-our-youth program—only when I faced them. Circumstances seemed to be saving me from facing these horrors on my first day of school; the scheduling going on in the gymnasium meant that Phys Ed classes had to assemble in the auditorium. For the moment it looked as if I was home free.

The auditorium was comparatively small and badly lighted. Rows of seats, which would accommodate about five hundred people, filled one large center section and two smaller side sections. There were a hundred or so girls scattered throughout the three sections. When the gymnasiums became available, the girls scheduled for this hour would be divided into three or four groups, each with a different teacher.

Urban's four female Phys Ed teachers were seated under bright lights at a long table on the stage. Flanking each was a pair of student lieutenants. When the previously described lieutenant had finished her announcement about new students signing in, a dozen girls put their books down on their chairs and marched up on the stage. I followed them and found myself waiting, under what felt like floodlights, center stage, while a lieutenant searched for my name on a twelve-page list. Finally she found it, checked me off, and gave a card with my name on it to the first gym teacher.

She glanced at me. "You take her in your class, Gert," she said, handing my card to the next gym teacher.

"Why can't you take her in yours?" asked Gert.

"Because I've got all these transfers from this morning," said teacher number one.

"Well, can't Jo take her in hers?" Gert turned to Jo. "Jo, do you have room in 5B?"

Jo looked up from her list, squinted in my direction, and shook her head from side to side. "I'm all filled unless Ackerman and Nugent switch to first lunch, and then they'll be in 4C. Why can't Mabel take her?"

Traffic had stalled behind me, but that fact didn't ruffle the teachers. Two of them looked exactly alike. They were all attractive, but spare and cold. The identical pair had brown Dutch-boy-cut hair, colorless eyes, good firm clear complexions, perfect figures, and remarkable posture. Their lieutenants were pretty, athletic, camp-counselor types—feet planted firmly on the ground, shoulders back, jaws set.

Eventually Mabel took me. "Okay, Tornabene, put your name here," she said, looking past me to the next girl. I was officially in gym class.

Amazing.

A few minutes later I was standing in the far right aisle, waiting to be given a seat assignment. A Negro girl leaning on the wall near me mumbled something in my direction. I couldn't understand her. "Excuse me," I said to her, "I didn't hear you. What did you say?"

56

She looked at me quickly. "Hey," she said, "are you a teacher?"

I shook my head no. "I didn't hear you," I mumbled. "Whatja want?"

She looked at me suspiciously. "A sticka gum."

I gave her a stick of gum and turned away.

When we were seated, I took out a mirror to see if I had aged in the last half hour. I hadn't, but I had paled considerably. Also, my hands were shaking. I took off my glasses to comb my hair. From my right came a high-pitched voice: "Hi, you're in my English class, aren't you?"

It was a girl I had noticed in English class because she was wearing a pair of gray-and-white dizzily plaid knee socks—one of the few pairs of knee socks of any kind I had seen worn in the school. Her name was Gretel. I smiled at her and said "Hi" in a high-pitched voice.

A girl in front of me swiveled around. She was quite pretty, but about thirty pounds overweight. She had large round green eyes with long lashes, a small nose with a straight bridge, a baby-doll mouth, straight white teeth. Her hair was blondish, short, full and well-styled. On top of it she had placed a huge bow that made her look a bit like a butterfly balloon in the Macy's Thanksgiving Day parade. She was immaculately groomed. Her name, as I learned shortly, was Cooky.

"Hey," she said, "you're the one that girl thought was a teacher, aren't you?"

"Yeah," I said. "Isn't that *funny?*"

She was now turned around completely in her chair, the better to appraise me. "Yo *do* look like a teacher," she said. "Your clothes are like a teenager, but your face is old. *Look, Gretel.* Look at her face. It's so *old.*"

I felt sick. Something had happened to the center of gravity. I was floating in the air and had no way to get my feet down. I held the mirror I was clutching up to my face but saw nothing in it.

"I don't think I look old," I stuttered. "WhydoyouthinkI lookold? Idon'tthinkIlookold."

Cooky continued staring at me, muttering like an art appraiser in front of a Rembrandt. "Old, yes. Hmmm. Yes, old."

Gretel was staring at me, too; I could feel it. I didn't move. Then I heard her cheerfully singsonging, "She doesn't look old, Cooky. You're crazy."

"You don't look old," she said to me. In a moment I found out how she could pronounce this with such sincerity. "I love your glasses," she exclaimed. "Can I try them on?"

She reached over and took my glasses, leaving me with naked eyes and the immediate necessity to point out how mild was my eye trouble. (It is on such small details as fake lenses that many a spy has found himself hoist.)

"How do they look on me?" Gretel asked, turning first to me and then to her mirror. "Oh, they're *cute*. Where did you get them? I never saw any like these."

"New York," I squeaked.

"Oh, are you from New York? So am I. Cooky, she's from New York."

Cooky remained impassive. She took one more permanent impression of my face and slowly returned to a normal position in her chair.

"Let me try on *your* glasses," I said to Gretel.

She handed them to me, giggling. "I'm terribly nearsighted," she said. It was one of the understatements of the year. I put on her glasses and dropped off the edge of the globe. The girl could barely see. I had found the ideal friend.

Gretel. Tall, skinny, working at being blond; pretty, really, when you looked beyond the thick glasses. She

58

wore the same clothes everyone else did, but with an offbeat air. She had long fingers, thin wrists, and heaps of bones connected by slack string. Her eyes were big and pale and heavily made up—though no more heavily than everyone else's eyes.

"How do you like it here?" she asked me.

"I guess I'll get used to it," I answered. "It's pretty, but I don't know anybody and it's hard to make friends."

"Oh, I know," said Gretel. "'But it will be all right, you'll see. I had the same thing when I came here two years ago. And then I met this boy and we went everywhere together and I met all his friends and everything was fine. It will happen to you, you'll see." Her voice was like a gentle pat on the hand.

"Who'd you eat with today?" she asked.

"No one," I lied.

"Gee, that's awful, to eat alone. Tomorrow maybe you could eat with us. Would you want to?"

"Gee, thanks, sure," I said.

"Okay," said Gretel. "You can bring a sandwich if you want to. Sometimes we do that."

Cooky turned around and addressed herself to Gretel: "I had such a good lunch today, you know? I had a seeded roll—French, you know? With cheese? A cupcake, an orange, and milk. It was *good*, really *good*." She turned back.

"Mm," said Gretel. She paused. Cooky moved an arm. Gretel spoke:

"Gerry called me up last night?" (Inflection straight up.) "And she said she dyed her hair *red?* So I look at her this morning and it's blond." (Inflection straight down.) Pause. Deep breath.

"You didn't call me last night."

Cooky: I didn't have time. I got to bed so late. You know, I need at least eight hours of sleep? I was going to go to bed at ten. *The Rogues* was on, but so *late*. All the new TV shows are on now. I started to go to bed at ten, brushed my teeth. And I forgot to put up my hair and it was eleven o'clock. I didn't get into bed until eleven-thirty.

Gretel: You know Mark, how he talks about everybody? *WELL*, boy, you should have heard him this morning talking about Fran and how they broke up and everything. He let everybody think she was going to have a baby, and I didn't think that was nice.

Cooky: Mm. Do you have any Blush with you?

Gretel: No. Do you have any light lipstick?

Cooky: I have white lipstick.

Gretel: I said *light*, not white. Do you have a mirror?

Cooky: Do I have a mirror? Naturally I have a mirror.

Cooky handed her mirror to Gretel, who put on powder and combed her hair. Then she returned the mirror, whereupon Cooky reached into a pocketbook the size of an overnight bag and removed enough cosmetics to make up the entire cast of *A Midsummer Night's Dream*. She squeezed some base out of a tube and applied it under her eyes and over her nose and chin. She relined her eyes with a black pencil. She put on another coat of mascara. She brushed her eyebrows with a tiny brush and extended them a hair or two with a light brown pencil. She artfully applied two shades of lipstick that added up to one invisible hue. Then she attacked her hair. First she gingerly removed the bow, then vigorously combed through her entire coiffure. Then she reteased it, a strand at a time. That done, she groped in the bag (when she reached into it her arm disappeared right up to the shoulder) and came up with an economy-size can of hair spray. She gave her hair a double blast, replaced the bow, and took a long look in her mirror.

Gretel said to me, "Tee-hee. Look at her. She does this

every gym class. Did you see her *pocket*book? Show her, Cooky. You're a nut, Cooky."

The show was over. Gretel once again focused (so to speak) on me. She asked what courses I was taking and looked briefly at my schedule. She commented only about public speaking. "Why are you taking that? I think you speak fine," she said. I told her my aunt thought it would help my shyness. She said, "Oh." Then she asked where I lived and I gave her a vague answer, mentioning the general area rather than the specific street. She said it wasn't far from where she lived.

Throughout this exchange, Gretel's eyes roved over the auditorium checking entrances, exits, dark corners, the ceiling, the floor, and the seats, row by row. Cooky's did the same. The two girls were like soldiers on night watch, straining for every sound, alert to every foreign move-ment. Whatever observations they made were telegraphed during conversational lulls: "Jen got her hair cut." Stop. "They didn't fix the chair Chuck broke yet." Stop. "Hey, the T is off that sign." Stop. "Judy's not here today." Stop.

One of Cooky's primary observations was that with a face as long as mine I should wear my hair shorter. She made it ten minutes after that last time she had looked at me. Gretel's final observation was that the clock was three minutes slow. It was, she noted on schedule, time to go. Cooky said to Gretel, "Call me tonight." Gretel said to me, "See ya in English tomorrow and don't forget about lunch." I said, "I don't know where my next class is." Gretel said, "C'mon, it's near my locker, I'll show ya." And away we went.

"Hi Tom, Hi Dot, HiBill, HiSam, HiJohn, HiBoo, HiLes, hihihi," said Gretel to 3,971 kids on the way up to the fourth floor where my class was. She apparently knew everyone in the school and I said so, in dialect of course: "Gee, you know *every*one. Golly."

61

"Oh, no I don't," said Gretel, shyly. She was pleased I had said so. "Do you have a locker?" she asked. I said I didn't. "C'mon," she said, "You can use mine."

I felt myself smile spontaneously for the first time that day. Gretel smiled, too.

I had made a friend. True, I had an old face, but I also had a young friend. I had listened to her talking with another young friend. At lunch, less than twenty-four hours away, I would meet more of her friends.

The plan was working.

# 7

FOR MOST ADULTS, the day would just be going into high gear at the hour I signed into Public Speaking (on time, it should be noted). For my classmates, the day was grinding to an end, and they showed it in mood and posture. They were so fidgety they couldn't sit still even for the normal duration of five minutes. Pity ye the teacher who has to make a point during the final hour of the school day. He must find a way to be more vital and interesting than the face of the clock over the blackboard.

The Public Speaking teacher of Urban High, a Mr. Roth, was blessedly endowed to meet this task. For one thing, he neither looked nor dressed like anybody's notion of a high school teacher, except a television producer's. He was in his early thirties, five feet nine, a perfect size 38. He had black hair cut à la Johnny Carson, a yacht-club tan on his sensitive face, and he was attired, if you please, in a navy-blue blazer, gray flannels, and black-rimmed eyeglasses of a type rarely spotted west of Madison Avenue.

For another thing, there was his manner.

"You are an unusual group or you would not be here,"

he said to the class, for openers. "Average students do not sign up for public speaking. I am not going to treat you as though you were average students. I am not going to tolerate noise like that I heard when I walked in here just now. You've had three days to settle down. From now on, when I close that door this class will begin. I will be the only one talking until you are invited to speak. Then you will speak clearly and distinctly a n d  s l o w l y  s o e v e r y o n e  c a n  u n d e r s t a n d  y o u."

He grinned unexpectedly. "Okay," he said, clapping his hands lightly together. "We understand each other, don't we? By the end of the week I intend to know each one of you very well. And I assure you you will also know me."

As Mr. Roth spoke, the meek trembled. There were only seventeen pupils present, and most of them looked as if they, too, were there because their counselors thought they were shy.

One boy and one girl smiled. Not at each other, smiled privately. The girl wore her hair up and pinioned with a fake chignon. Her eyebrows were plucked to a fare-thee-well, which was also what her nails were manicured to. She sat straight, without leaning against the back of her chair, the way English ladies sit for high tea. If I had seen her anywhere else, I would have guessed her age to be twenty-seven.

The smiling boy was equally unusual. He was tall, tweedy, and shabby. He wore a charcoal-gray jacket with the sleeves pushed up to show six inches of shirt-sleeve, a pale gray sweater, and plain gray slacks. There were paint blots on his shoes. His hair was long, brown, thick, and curly. He looked a little like Abe Lincoln in Illinois, and I couldn't help staring at him, making bets with myself that within two years he'd have a beard and a cause.

64

My mistake was that I was staring instead of paying attention to Mr. Roth. When I tuned him in again, he sounded unmistakably unfriendly.

"You, miss, stand up," he was saying.

When I turned to find out whom he was about to behead, I found him standing near my own desk, looking straight at me. I blushed.

"Yes, you," he said. "Stand up."

I stood up.

"How long have you been at Urban High School?"

I was silent.

"Have you been here long enough to know you are not allowed to chew gum in this school?"

I shook my head no.

"Oh, you haven't? Well, then, tell us how long you have been here." Mr. Roth smiled at the rest of the class.

"One day," I said.

Mr. Roth was annoyed. He shrugged and walked quickly to his desk, looked down at it and then back up in my direction. I remained standing.

"Kindly deposit your chewing gum in the wastepaper basket," he said. I did so feeling more embarrassed than I had felt in at least a decade.

Mr. Roth sighed with exasperation. "This is a class in public speaking," he said. "We will have no gum-chewing. I will flunk anyone I see chewing gum in this class, from this day on. Do you understand that, miss?" Though I couldn't pick up my head to verify that this question was directed at me, I nodded.

After a dramatically quiet moment, Mr. Roth announced that he would spend the period conducting individual interviews for the purpose of analyzing speech defects. He would do three or four such interviews each day, he said, taking each of us in turn, alphabetically. Then he called a Mr. Abbey to his desk.

I'd forgotten how strong a role in one's fate is played by the first initial of one's last name.

Throughout their entire school years, an Abbey and a Tornabene can sit in the same room and yet have two different environments, face two entirely different configurations of circumstance. If, for instance, I had been Miss Abbey at Urban, I would have had an individual speech analysis my first day of school. I would have had to sit at Mr. Roth's desk, six inches from those black-rimmed glasses, and read aloud while he listened and watched. As it was, I had a few days to prepare for this event, or find a way to avoid it.

Our speech homework for the following day was to catch a news commentator on television and make a report on his method of delivery. Then we were to observe a television commercial and make a report on its method of delivery. We would be required to read our reports aloud in class before handing them in.

Shortly before class ended, Mr. Roth told us that we were to report to our home rooms before leaving school. We would do so all week, he said, and maybe longer, depending upon how long it would take to clear up the programming problems created by the unexpectedly large enrollment.

Hearing this, one boy in class groaned. Mr. Roth walked over to the row of desks where he was sitting. "What's on your mind, young man?" he inquired.

The boy blushed.

"No, I mean it. What's on your mind? In this class we don't make noises, we speak. Tell us what's bothering you."

At which point the bell rang and everyone ran like hell out the door.

The purpose of home room was the same as the assemblies held back in the days when an entire school popula-

66

tion could fit into one auditorium; to make general announcements. Mass assemblies are impossible in most high schools today. Many high schools don't even bother with home room periods; they deliver printed messages to students as the words roll off the school printing press, or they use a public address system.

Recently I visited a school using the latter method. In the middle of a class period a voice would blare out of a nearly invisible speaker in the wall: ATTENTION B TWELVES. ATTENTION B TWELVES. THE RESULTS OF YOUR CLASS ELECTIONS ARE NOW IN. RONNY STARK IS YOUR NEW PRESIDENT. REPEAT: RONNY STARK IS YOUR NEW PRESIDENT. OTHER OFFICERS WILL BE ANNOUNCED AFTER RONNY TAKES OFFICE. REPEAT: RONNY STARK IS YOUR NEW PRESIDENT. THAT IS ALL. The students were so conditioned to this system that when a message came for B Twelves the B Elevens didn't even hear it. There was never a warning signal when an announcement was to be made. The loud speaker just coughed and began: NOW HEAR THIS. ATTENTION. ATTENTION. For those at whom the announcement was aimed, all work ceased until the voice did. Very weird.

The home room teacher to whom I had been assigned was quite pretty in a Lee Remick sort of way. She was five feet eight in her spike-heeled pumps, had warm brown hair, swept up, and big brown eyes. She wore a skirt and sweater prettily, and an engagement ring and a wedding ring. She was about my real age.

The kids in class seemed to be very fond of her. They were, in fact, all over her. They called to her from around the room: "Mrs. Brown, why don't we all get our bus tickets together so we'll know when we have them?" "Hey, Mrs. Brown, let's have a pizza party like we had last year."

Everyone in class knew everyone else; this was their

67

second year with Mrs. Brown and with each other. It was all very *gemütlich*—if you were in. If you were not in, you might well feel in that room like a Hatfield at a McCoy cookout.

There were two of us not in: a Negro boy from Chicago, and myself. Mrs. Brown looked at our schedules and directed us to stand by the windows. "All the desks are taken," she explained. After she closed the door she told me I could use the stool in the corner. She said nothing to the Negro boy.

The main announcement was that there was to be a football game Friday afternoon, and maybe a dance afterward. One of the boys in our room was the captain of the cheerleaders. He stood up and said he hoped we would all show at the football game.

Further announcements, made by Mrs. Brown, concerned the election of officers scheduled for the next day, an emergency call for musicians for the band, and new times set for the regular meetings of several extracurricular activities. Mrs. Brown asked if she'd forgotten anything, and a slim little girl stood up to remind us all not to forget to bring our dollars for our student activities cards. She also volunteered to be in charge of getting city bus tickets for the class. Mrs. Brown thanked her, and then it was 3:10, class dismissed.

My God, I felt strange walking out of Urban, a part of the young mob happily sprung from class. I felt stranger than I'd felt all day, older, more tired, more alone. Out on the street, with all the kids bounding around me, laughing and shouting and talking and strolling together two by two, three by three, crowd by crowd. I felt more freakish. And I was sure I looked it. Without the cover the school building offered, I was certain the contrast between my old face and young clothes was glaringly obvious.

Most discomforting of all, I didn't know the way back to Bess's. We had been so anxious to get me into school, we'd forgotten to discuss how to get me out of it. Mrs. Brown had been generous enough to point the way to my bus stop. Somebody, she said, would direct me from there; but no one did.

There were, perhaps, sixty youngsters at my bus stop. A man from the bus company also stood there, trying to keep order. Several different buses stopped at that corner, and as they did, he called out their numbers and lined up the children getting on them. He told me, when I asked, that I needed a No. 3 bus, and then tried to recruit someone taking a No. 3 to stay with me until I got to the point where I had to transfer to another bus.

"Who'll help this nice little girl?" he shouted, repeatedly. No one answered. When I tried to get him to stop asking, he told me not to be "so snotty." Finally, he exacted a promise of help from a red-faced boy who promptly missed his bus because I was afraid to get on it. When I had stepped toward the door there was such a crush I was sure I was going to be trampled to death, so I stepped back and just let the doors close in my face.

Two grim bus rides and one long uphill climb later, I dropped my notebook, speech book, and Spanish book on the floor of Bess's living room, and headed for the bathroom, the bar, and a cigarette, in that order. Bess was not home yet. I sat down to wait for her and then, toting a large vodka-on-the-rocks, wandered compulsively to the mirror in the front hall.

There was only one reason why I had spent a successful first day as a student in Urban High School, and I realized it the moment I faced my reflection. No adult I had met had looked at my face. The Dean of Girls, my guidance counselor, my teachers—all they had seen of me was a small, fuzzy shape they assumed to be a teenager. Why,

69

after all, should they have thought I was anything else? I had come to register in their school, just another kid. They had looked at me the way they look at any other teenager, which is to say, not at all. Maybe they never would scrutinize me. Maybe my skirt and sweater were a magic cloak. Or maybe my shield was only the confusion of the first days of school.

While I was up, staring at myself, I also realized that I should never have cut my hair into bangs. I would have been much better camouflaged if I had just parted it in the middle and let it fall over my face like draperies. The way it was, with my bangs stopping short of my eyeballs, left too much age showing. I got a pair of scissors and tried to make enough out of my sidelocks to cover my crow's-feet. It worked: no wrinkles showed at all—until I moved my head.

So I poured myself another vodka.

When Bess arrived home I was stretched out, slightly crocked, watching either Huntley or Brinkley deliver the news.

"I'm sorry I'm so late," she shouted from the foyer. "How'd it go? How'd you do? What happened?"

She bounded into the living room and stopped short at the head of the couch. "Are you watching *television?*" she asked incredulously.

"No," I said. "I'm doing my speech homework."

"Oh," said Bess.

"It's all right. You can turn it off. I'll do my homework later."

She turned off the machine.

"Somebody said I have an old face," I told her. And then I went over the day, inch by inch.

"Now *I* have a little news," she said when I'd finished. "Your guidance counselor called to inform me you're a very disturbed child. She said I'm not to worry, though, because she's going to keep an eye on you."

70

Bess paused to let me absorb this, and then started to laugh. Once she started, she couldn't stop. She folded in half. She roared. She fell in her chair and howled. She rocked, she rolled. Tears dripped out of her eyes.

"What is it?" I hollered over her guffaws. "What are you laughing at?"

She took a gulp of air and wiped her eyes. "I was just thinking," she said. "What if they send you to the school psychiatrist?"

# 8

I CONSIDER my collective experiences at Urban High a succession of events that couldn't possibly have happened but did. Among the most astonishing and improbable, to me, was the ease and speed with which I was able to become part of a gang (for lack of a better word) of girls. Gretel was the reason I was accepted, but that, too, was improbable. How strange that a sixteen-year-old girl should become my unquestioning sponsor. It was like Cinderella sending her Fairy Godmother to the ball. From the moment Gretel rescued me in gym class I became her friend, and thus the friend of all her friends. Just like that.

I met them during a lunch hour which began, as did all my lunch hours, with a beauty routine in the last minutes of English class and a "Hi, did you bring a sandwich? Come on, we've got to stop at my locker," from Gretel. We were always late eating because our English class was four floors above the cafeteria and Gretel had a vital message for at least 70 per cent of the people she met on the way down. Sample message: "Hi, Normalou. Have you seen Sandy? Tell her to call me tonight, will you? How's Carl? Listen, I've gotta run but I'll see you in Spanish. Okay?"

Gretel also was subject to traumas, which, when they hit, would abruptly halt our march. Anything might cause one—a lost notebook, a fallen paper, an old boyfriend. The traumas were totally unpredictable and often incomprehensible. The one on our first lunch was brought on by a teacher who passed us on the landing of the third floor. As she went by, Gretel gasped and grabbed my arm.

"Oh my God, did you see that?" she said.

"What?" I inquired.

"Mrs. Cramer. I have that suit. *That same suit.* Oh no. Oh my God. I just bought it. That plaid suit. It cost twenty-six dollars. What'll I do? What'll I *do?* Oh my God." She repeated the last two lines on every other step.

The stairs were fairly well emptied out by the time Gretel and I got on them. If they hadn't been, we surely would have been heaved over a landing.

Gretel wasn't bothered by the stampedes, though. She wasn't even bothered by the one at the door of the cafeteria. She elbowed her way right through the middle of it. Once inside the doors, she charged, shoulders back, head high, straight to the table her gang always occupied.

"Sit here," she said to me, pulling two stools out from under the table. "I'm going for a hot dog."

"Bring me some milk," yelled a girl at mid-table.

Gretel stopped to collect seven cents for the carton of milk, and yelled back at me to see if I wanted anything. I likewise requested milk, and likewise paid in advance for it. It was important to pay in advance, I learned. The kids I got to know never offered to lay out cash for each other because borrowed money was rarely returned. To advance money for a friend was to carry the friend, and no one did that. It was not a matter of being sporty or cheap. The girls all carried the same amount of money and had the same expenses. To be a sport was to be a fool. If you blew the crowd to potato chips you would receive no

73

more than a puzzled shrug for your trouble. I know because I did it. I shouldn't have.

When Gretel returned with the milk, she introduced me to Billy and Angela. We were joined by Kelly and Roxanne. (Today's teenagers have very exotic names.) A girl named Avis stood nearby. This was the hub of the gang. Other girls moved in and out and around our table but they were peripheral friends. Cooky, whom I met earlier with Gretel, was an overlap. She was Gretel's friend but a member of a different gang.

"Hi. You're from New York. Gretel told me. Hi."

"Hi. When'd you get here? What grade are you in?"

"Hi. Are you from New York City or Long Island? I know somebody in Hempstead. My cousin. But I don't think you'd know him. He's older."

"Hi," I said, and Billy, Angela, Kelly, and Roxanne smiled.

Billy was a girl notable for her vocabulary, which came straight out of the foxholes of World War II. She was about five feet five, had short, wavy, dark blond hair, blue eyes, a good solid figure, and ferociously flailing arms. When I met her she wore a plaid, pleated skirt, a dark green blazer, a short-sleeved white Orlon sweater, stockings and flats. She wore variations of that theme every day. The odd note in her getup was her eye makeup, which she wore in greater quantity than anyone else at the table. Most of the girls wore black or brown eye makeup, but Billy used blue liner, blue shadow, and blue mascara. She never appeared without it. The sight was as startling as a blue leaf on a stalk of celery.

Angela was a fawn, fragile and lovely, with exceptional taste in clothes. She probably weighed no more than ninety-eight, though she was Billy's height. She had not one curve to her frame. She was all neck and eyes, a physical fact emphasized by her hair, which was pinned

74

up in a way that left wisps on her neck and forehead. The first day I saw her she had on an outfit I had seen in a fashion magazine—even to the little-heeled patent leather shoes on her feet. She always looked that new and shiny. She didn't always act that way.

Kelly was fifteen and three quarters years old, the youngest member of the gang. She and Roxanne were best friends and resembled each other abstractly. Whether the resemblance was the cause or effect of their friendship was difficult to determine. There was no real physical similarity, rather an aura of unity, as though they were head and tail of the same coin. They were very bizarre-looking—a result, Gretel told me, of their having "gone English" together. They had identical short, geometric, banged hairdos, Kelly's brown, Roxanne's black. They wore short short skirts and slim black boots. I have since become accustomed to their style, as has the rest of the world, but at the time they looked to me like a pair of moon girls.

In addition to being American mods, Kelly and Roxanne were something else I had never encountered before: Beatle nuts. Certainly I knew there were millions of such creatures around, but when I discovered a pair of them in my own circle, I felt as if I'd captured two whooping cranes in a butterfly net. Because I was so green it took me a couple of days to get the Beatle thing; the hip would have known it in a glance. Each wore a sign: Roxanne's was a pair of huge sunglasses worn in and out of doors; Kelly's a short trench coat, sported in all her waking hours. Both talked Beatle talk. Both breathed and ate the Beatles. Both took a shot of "I Love You, Yeh, Yeh, Yeh" every day, like a fix.

They sustained their habit through Avis, whose relationship with the gang apparently began and ended with her role of Beatle pusher. I wondered, as I observed her, what she'd do for friends when Kelly and Roxanne finally got an overdose, which they no doubt have by now.

Poor oversized, unwashed, unattractive Avis. She spent her entire allowance on fan magazines with Beatle pictures in them and carried new ones with her nearly every lunch hour. She never ate, never even sat down at the table. She just hovered around, waiting for the right moment to say "Look, Kelly, here's a picture of Ringo in bed," of "Look, look, Kelly, Ringo wears a medal." Try as Kelly might to ignore her, she had to look. After Kelly looked, Roxanne looked. Once they looked, Avis had them.

But it all didn't happen at once or in one day. My initiation opened with an attack by Billy on a local candidate for mayor of the city. The tirade was provoked by Gretel's presence. It got started, in the first place, because I noticed the election stickers many of my classmates had on their notebooks.

"Where d'ya get them?" I asked Billy. She belonged to a political club, she told me, and offered me one of the dozen she was carrying. As I was gluing it on my notebook, she told me Gretel was for the third party candidate, a well-publicized far-right extremist. Gretel blushed. "Are you?" I asked. She nodded. Whereupon something known as "all hell" broke loose and everybody started screaming at Gretel. Billy leaped to her feet, wildly waving her arms.

"He's crazy, he's crazy," she half laughed, half shrieked. "That man is *crazy*, I tell you."

Gretel shrugged and fingered her carton of milk. At the other end of the table a girl who looked like Angela, only bulkier, jumped to her feet and joined Billy in her arm flapping. By this time, Billy had the curious attention of a few boys. She saw them looking at her and took a deep breath. Then, with all the subtlety of Barbra Streisand

76

playing to the crowd, she turned her lecture into a galvanizing performance. She tossed back her hair, wiped her brow, took a gulp of milk and a bite of sandwich and proclaimed across the cafeteria:

"He's *crazy*. I read a book about him last night. Do you know what he said about the U.N.?"

"I don't care," Gretel said softly.

"He's *nuts!*" shouted Billy. "He's crazy," echoed the other standing girl. Then they sat down and shared a cupcake.

As soon as I could hear, I asked Gretel why she favored this man.

She answered, "Because he'll stop them. Somebody's got to stop them. If we let them go any further they'll be telling us what to do. My father said so."

"Who are *they?*"

"The colored people."

The discussion ended there. I didn't know what more to say. Gretel was beyond my research. I had read only about the liberal, idealistic teenager who sang "We Shall overcome" marching to Washington and points south. At home I had met only Freedom Riders or kids who were ashamed of their parents for permitting the downtrodden to stay that way. But I was to learn that many other pupils at Urban—some as gentle-natured as Gretel, some not—shared her feelings about "them."

Talk went on and on and on at the table. In the comparatively quiet seconds between topics, I became aware of the nearly intolerable din in the cafeteria. As lunch hour progressed, and meals were gulped and shredded, the noise became more and more jolting. Trays were being slammed together and stools knocked around; dirty silverware and dishes were being heaped in piles by kids hurrying for exits. Laughing, shouting, whistling, and a full range of discordant sounds filled every cubic inch of the low-ceilinged room. It was feeding time at the zoo, but from *inside* the monkeys' cage.

"Hey," Gretel shouted across the table to Billy. "You know what I saw in the *hall?* You know that French teacher who came last year?"

"Yeah."

"Well, she has on my plaid suit. You know that black-and-white one I just bought? That one. The new one."

"Doesn't that piss the hell out of you?" said Billy. "God, I *hate* that. And a teacher yet. Shit, Gretel, what are you gonna do?"

"I could die."

"Shit, I'll bet you could. Boy."

Down at the end of the table a positively beautiful, tanned, golden-haired, perfectly poised girl stood giggling with two other likewise long-haired and bronzed girls. At her right was a tall, golden-haired, bronzed boy. My gang was giving them all a very cool appraisal.

"Who's that?" I asked.

"Richy Allen." said Billy. "He's got a blue T-bird. His mother has a yellow one."

"No, I mean the girl. Who's she?"

"Georgia Katz," said Gretel.

"Georgia's getting to be a snob," said Roxanne to nobody in particular.

"She goes steady with a guy in college," Gretel told me. Then she'd had enough of Georgia.

"Do you go steady?" I asked Gretel.

"Not any more," she answered. "I was going with this boy for a year and a half. We just broke up. Kelly just broke up, too. Everybody broke up this summer."

"How long did you go with him?" I asked Kelly.

"Seven months, three days, and four hours," she answered.

"Hey, Roxanne, did you eat all the potato chips?"

"No, beast, here's your old potato chips."

Phrases crisscrossed down the table: "No, *honest.*" "He *did?*" "They *were?*" She *is?*" "What shit." "Hey, who's going for cake?"

"Listen, let's go." "C'mon, I'm going outside."

The warden came by and blew his whistle. Gretel stuck her tongue out at him. Billy stood up. "See ya outside," she announced. "C'mon, Kelly, move your ass."

After eating, the gang always gathered in a space in the upper right corner of the compound. It belonged to them for the duration of their junior year and was the best space available to juniors except for the turf restricted to Georgia Katz and her gang. Only a few kids sat on the available low wall. The other hundreds were on their feet —though rarely both feet at the same time; one foot always stayed in motion: toe turned in, heel up, knee swinging; heel down, toe up, ankle turning; toe down, heel up, knee bent, then shift—other toe down, heel up, knee bent. Now both knees bent and moved back and forth as in the frug. That was for the girls, the leg motion. The boys used their arms and their hands. Mostly to shove each other around.

The look of lunch hour outside was the look of a huge ballet with choreography by Agnes de Mille. Group within group moved in various dance rhythms: now a reel, now a gavotte, now a twist. A mazurka, a cakewalk, a laughing two-step.

"Hey," Roxanne said, waltzing at me. "Do you like the Beatles?"

That was before I knew she was a Beatle nut but after I was aware that I would be given impromptu test questions. I thought it over.

"Yes," I mumbled. If it was the wrong answer, I could

change it to "No" a little louder, a device I'd picked up from my classmates.

"We do too." Roxanne smiled, including Kelly. "We went to see them at the airport."

"Gee, did you?" I exclaimed. "Did you really see them?" Right foot forward, left foot back, cha-cha-cha.

"Yes, honest. We waited seven hours. And Kelly almost touched Ringo." Shuffle, shuffle. Mashed potato.

"You're kidding!" I screamed, doing a Lindy.

"No, honest," Roxanne panted. "I'm not kidding. We went out to the airport by bus, and we waited in the rain and everything, and oh, their plane was late, and then it *landed* and it was *sooo* tough. Wasn't it, Kelly? Didn't we?"

"Oh yes," said Kelly, sneaking a meringue.

"Did you see the movie?" I asked.

"Oh yes," said Roxanne. "Wasn't it great? We saw it four times. Which one do you like?"

"Well, I think, well, Ringo," I said.

"Me too," said Kelly.

Behind us, two girls sitting on the wall were wondering what they were going to have for supper.

"We had lamb chops three times last week," one moaned.

"Yeah," sympathized her friend. "I dread Sundays. My mother makes a ham and we have it all week."

"I suppose we'll have a lamb thing tonight, too," said the first girl.

"Yeah," said the second.

Gretel was off doing a Virginia reel with Billy and Angela.

"Hey, Alicia's back," she hollered to Kelly. "Did you see her?" She smiled at me. I smiled back.

"Lyn, c'mon," she said, do-se-doing to my side. "It's time for gym class."

80

And so it was.

"Call me tonight," said Billy to Gretel. "Call me to-night," said Gretel to Roxanne. "Call ya tonight," said Roxanne to Kelly. "Call ya later," said Kelly to Angela. "I'll call ya tonight," said Avis to all. And off we went, Gretel and I, scraping our heels in a parting flamenco, waving goodbye to our friends.

# 9

They all began the same, all the seven-hour days from Monday to Friday, with the clicking sound of doorstops being released up and down the halls, and then reverberating whangs as the doors were slammed shut. Outside in the courtyard a group of sweatered boys carrying musical instruments huddled together, forming a citizens' army band. One of the boys raised his arm, and another started a slow drum roll. Behind closed doors all over the building, home room teachers nodded and students got to their feet. Then they all stood, still and solemn, while the band outside painfully rendered "The Star-Spangled Banner." On the last note, teachers placed hand to heart and led their classes in reciting the Pledge of Allegiance, after which, with much scuffing of chairs, the morning was under way.

Some days stayed the same, too, from morning to mid-afternoon. It sounds crazy to call any school days of such an elderly low eleven "normal" and "routine," but some were, and maybe I had to be a little bit crazy to find them so. It is a fact that at times at Urban my thoughts stripped down to the basics of teenage concern: friends and teachers, teachers and friends, sometimes without my realizing it. Sometimes I didn't know until I typed my notes at night that during the day my world had been a totally subjective teenage one—a big Shasta daisy from which I slowly plucked petals, reciting, "He loves me, she loves me not; I love her, I love him not."

Home room teacher, Mrs. Brown, I just plain hated in a plain, unadulterated adolescent way. She loved me not, and, in case I had forgotten, I remembered every day in her home room what it's like for a kid to be on a teacher's shit list.

I think she had it in for me on sight, but I'm not sure. She had it in for the Negro boy who had signed in with me, too. We were the only transfer students in her group, and she seemed to be punishing both of us, equally, for being new and superfluous. She never did introduce us to the class, never tried to find us a place to sit, never included us in her announcements. Because we had no desks and had to stand against the wall in front of the room, we rarely saw anything but her back. Twice, the Negro boy found a stool for me to sit on, and I took it because he had gotten it for me, though it was easier to stand than to sit balancing books on my lap.

On one of the days I sat on that stool, Mrs. Brown managed to turn me into the class dunce and fix my chances, but good, of getting to know anybody in home room. That was either the start or the climax of our peculiar relationship; I don't know enough about the lady's psyche to say which.

It was the morning of class elections. The fact that elections were going to be held had been announced the day before, and the students were perking on a high flame. They came into the room bubbling about who would vote for whom, and they could hardly wait for the Pledge to end to make their nominations. Two students were to be nominated for each office (president, vice-president, secretary, treasurer, and student council representative), and then the class would cast votes for one officer at a time by raising a hand while the nominee in question hid his eyes. I remembered that voting method from grade school; somebody should have outlawed it since then. About three kids voted securely for their friends and the rest of the room followed the leaders. One candidate is always a shoo-in; the other gets the vote of the person who nominated him, plus maybe one or two other buddies' votes.

Since everybody in Mrs. Brown's established group knew the candidates, the voting proceeded without any preliminaries. The candidates didn't have to stand up, or wave, or be identified in any other way. I considered myself strictly a spectator at the election. I didn't know anyone running and it never occurred to me to vote.

As I watched the election, somewhat amused by the game of follow the first voter, I noticed Mrs. Brown watching me. At one moment she was watching me while I was watching her, so I gave her a bright smile. She didn't return it.

When the voting ended there was a burst of excited chatter in the room. Mrs. Brown cut in on it in a dead, cold voice, with "Let's have quiet!" The chatter stopped instantly. All eyes turned to Mrs. Brown.

"Some people in here aren't voting," she said, "and that's up to them, but I think they ought to raise their hands so we can all see who they are. We shall go over the voting again.

"All those who want Nino Mangiacavallo for president, raise their hands."

She counted slowly up and down the rows.

"Thirty-one. Is that it? All right. All those who want Bobby Lee for president . . . raise their hands."

Six hands went up. One was the Negro boy's.

84

"Six. Is that right? Six? Now, then. All those abstaining, raise their hands."

I raised my hand. The class stared at me. Without looking my way, Mrs. Brown said, "One. Is that right? One?" The class nodded mechanically, now staring at the teacher. She stage-waited and then went on, asking for a show of hands for Calvin Haines for vice-president.

It took her forever to count, and when she finished, she recounted. "Bitch," I thought. I couldn't believe she was going to continue. I couldn't grasp the reason. Maybe she thought I'd vote, in penance, by the time she reached student council representative. Maybe I should have. But I couldn't.

The class was as fascinated as a crowd at a hanging. I was shaking, partly with humiliation, partly with frustration. I was responding to my own plight like an indignant parent wondering why her little girl was being mistreated. Once again I was being singled out and made a fool of. Why? Was I being hazed, like "Let's see what the new kid can take"? That was a possibility. There was another: there may have been an air of assurance about me not usually found in high school juniors unless they're looking for trouble. Mrs. Brown may have sniffed out something that threatened her.

Whatever the reason, by the time I had publicly abstained four times, she and I were mortal enemies. She looked satisfied. I was the class pariah. The situation should have struck me as funny—considering that I was older than she was—but it didn't. What was happening to me in that room didn't happen to suburban matrons very often, but it happened to real kids every day. There was nothing I could do except philosophize.

Mr. Goodman's American history class was blessedly safe. Every time I entered it I thought of the scene from the second *Hunchback of Notre Dame* when Charles

85

Laughton secures Maureen O'Hara in the church and holds back the villains with cries of "Sanctuary!" History class was like Mr. Goodman; so ordered, so predictable, so dispassionate, so . . . school days. My sanctuary.

Mr. Goodman had systems. There was, for instance, his grading system. He detailed it even before we got our textbooks. He graded, he said, on a bell-shaped curve, which he drew on the blackboard. The way he drew it, it had a wide plateau on the top. Nearly everyone in class was going to fit on the plateau, he said, or else.

He had a system for assignments. They would be given at the start of the period. If they were written assignments, they were to be turned in in a standard way: on three-ring, lined notebook paper 8½ by 11, with your name (last first) in the upper right-hand corner, your section, your seat number (we were seated alphabetically and given numbers); on the next line, the date; under that, the subject of the assignment as he would write it on the board.

He believed in outlines, he said. Oulines served a purpose. He would outline all his lectures.

The daily routine of his class would be as follows: During the first five minutes he would take the roll and we would read our history books. No talking. None. Then he would give a fifteen- or twenty-minute lecture on the reading we had done the night before. Then maybe there would be an oral quiz out of the assignment or the lecture. If not, we would start our next reading assignment. There would be a *big* test at midterm. If you missed that, you had to take the makeup test, which was much more difficult. The class had one term paper to do, and the outline for it was due before the second report card period. We would get our first report cards on October 23.

As Mr. Goodman spoke, he wrote his key words on the

blackboard. Really *key* key words, he underlined, and with such vigor that one out of every three strokes shattered the chalk he was using. When his words turned into a lecture, he outlined what he was saying on the blackboard. For example, his first lecture on the meaning of history chalked up like this:

I. Introduction
    A. Definition—History
        1. Greek—istor—knowing
        2. Latin—historia—a learning by inquiry
        3. English—an account of what has happened
        4. The branch of knowledge that deals systematically with the past; a *recording, analyzing, coordination,* and *explaining* of past events
    B. Why
        1. Understand the present
        2. Experience
        3. *Predict* the *future*—ultimate goal of all knowledge

My reaction to Mr. Goodman and his systems was different from my classmates'. Whereas I found him tranquilizing, they found him numbing. I have never seen an audience so uniformly bored. They walked through the door yawning. They went passively to their desks and opened their notebooks. They took down all key words and outlines without folding, tearing, or spindling their notepaper. When they weren't taking notes they did math homework or doodled (BOO! read the back of the seat in front of me, and in fine print: "TOOT," "Steve," "JUDY," "shit." "See page 57," read the ball-point scribble on the fly leaf of my textbook. "F.U.," said page 57.) When they weren't doodling, they read. Some of them, mostly boys, read *Lord of the Flies,* and some, mostly girls, lip-read copies of *True Love*, *True Story*, and *True Romances* they had secreted in their notebooks. One morning the girl on my right finished an entire feature called "I'm Ashamed of My Mother." The next day she read "My Best Friend Stole My Baby," and on the next, "We Defied the World to Adopt This Child." After that, she caught me reading over her shoulder and hid her magazines.

Mr. Goodman did not seem to notice the various activities his class engaged in every day. He did not relate to the class as a whole at all. He was like an actor in a theater-in-the-round, skilled at avoiding eye contact with the audience in his lap. The only clue to the fact that he was, indeed, aware that his pupils were not concentrating on him was the way he followed all his instructions with a threat. He nearly always let his class know precisely what would happen if they didn't heed his words. When, for instance, he informed us that we were to have our textbooks covered within forty-eight hours, he described not only what he would accept as a book cover, but also what would happen to anyone who didn't obey. He had a negative point system, he said. It was elaborate and irrevocable. Anyone not covering his book got five negative points. Ten negative points and your grade dropped a notch. Negative points would also be given to those who didn't complete assignments, those who talked, those who were tardy, and so on. No one doubted that Mr. Goodman would make good his threats. Everyone knew what to expect from him at all times. Wherever he was, the weather was always the same.

Nearly every day at 10:10 A.M., a student messenger jerked open the door of my study hall room, took five quick steps in, dropped a packet of papers on the teacher's desk, whirled, took five more quick steps, and disappeared out the door. The first few times she appeared I thought I

88

was hallucinating. And even after I became certain she was real, I couldn't stop being astonished by the sight of her.

Her hair was two feet tall. She was small and slim and had all the appendages customarily found on a human being, but her black hair was two feet tall. Somehow she had managed to wrap all the hair on the crown of her head straight up into a stiff cylinder that looked like nylon thread on a huge bobbin. In order to defeat the law of gravity, which would never allow such a thing to stay in the air, she secured the bobbin with a fully exposed, three-inch metal hair clip. The rest of her hair hung straight to her shoulders, where it suddenly flipped up like a winter wave hitting a beach. When she walked, and even when she tossed her head, not a hair moved in any direction. Every time I saw her I gasped. Then I sat and pondered how she got out of her house in the morning looking like that. I would have given two white immies and a set of gold jacks to have seen her mother. And okay, forgetting her mother—what did she herself see when she looked in the mirror? A brain that could invent such a structure could not be all addled. But what was going on in it?

I ruminated frequently on such matters in study hall. I was grateful for the time there, and so, apparently, was everyone else in the room. The students were very quiet and kept their eyes on textbooks and notebooks through the entire hour. The teacher, too, was casually busy. He placed us at every other desk so we couldn't whisper to each other, and stayed as remote as a policeman in a lightly traveled tunnel.

Because he was so detached, I felt safe in approaching him from time to time. One day when I felt particularly worried about my tenure at Urban High, I asked him when the school might get my prior school records.

"We send at once for them," he said. "Where are you

89

from? New York? Well, the office must have written to the Board of Regents for your grades. They should be here soon."

If I had been looking for an excuse to panic, I got it. I hadn't thought about the Board of Regents. As a matter of fact, since I never went to school in New York, I didn't even know there was such a thing. I had heard of "taking Regents" and knew this was a trying procedure, but I didn't know if the Board of Regents really was as omniscient as it always sounded. I could only hope that among the four hundred transfer students who registered with me, there were enough from New York to keep the Board of Regents too busy to learn about my nonexistence.

Four hundred transfer students. An amazing figure. If we had had three when I went to high school, it would have been a lot. Four hundred relocated families. Four hundred kids trying to adjust to coming in on the middle of things—and the same was going on all over the country. How tractable those thousands of children would have to be. Two New York girls I met one day in gym class told me that junior year was the worst possible year to enter a new school environment. Sophomore year, they commented, was the year of finding niches; everybody was new to high school in sophomore year. Senior year was a time of privilege; a new senior could get by on seniority alone; seniors were regarded by everyone else in school as *years* older than juniors. But juniors—they had to have friends and the familiar; they had to be established, or they were lost. It would take them months to make friends and get invited to parties, and maybe they never would be accepted at all, except by other transfers.

. The one way a new student could make a quick assimilation was through the irresistible force of good looks. A "groovy-looking" guy, a cute girl, had very minor social problems regardless of where they were from or how recently. Pamela, the girl in my study hall whom I had tried to befriend, was a case in point. She was just in from Texas, and she was, by high school standards, adorable. Her braces and her adolescent complexion were no hindrance among her peers. She had a fresh, frothy look about her that other kids love, and an inexhaustible wardrobe of matching pastel skirts, sweaters, and shoes. One day she would wear all pink and look like a strawberry milk shake; another day she would wear all yellow and look like a lemon soda.

During the first fire drill at school, I had seen her standing alone in the street, three or four paces removed from the rest of her class. By second fire drill, which occurred during study hall, she was surrounded by boys so agog they looked as if they were asking for her autograph. By the end of the first week of school, there were always boys waiting for her after class. Once she had boys waiting for her, she had girls waiting for her. No average-looking girl could say the same.

Another thing Pamela could get away with because she was pretty was her "foreign" wardrobe. It didn't matter that her pastel skirts and sweaters were not normal on the Urban scene. A girl with her appeal could take her time acquiring a local uniform. On the other hand, the New York girls I talked to needed a whole new wardrobe—really needed it, and yesterday. They were suffering mightily in their Eastern togs. I met them, in fact, through their agony. I was in the locker room before gym class and one of them walked up to me and said, "You're from New York, aren't you?" I asked her how she knew that. She answered, sighing, "Your Pappagallos. Nobody out here wears them. I've got five pairs. God."

In addition to meditating, I also went exploring in study hall. As soon as I felt secure with the teacher, I requested written permission to go to the lavatory (now there's a nice old word) and set out determined to find it. Once not too long ago, I spent a weekend with friends in a charming New England village and on Sunday decided to explore it thoroughly on my own. I drove up every little dirt road off the main street, warming to the sights, until I turned into a tree-lined street that ended, without warning, in the town dump. By the time I had made a U-turn, I had learned more about the townsfolk than I cared to know.

I had precisely the same experience when I pushed open the unmarked door to Urban's second-floor john for the exclusive use of female students.

The walls of the room were painted corpse-gray, the doors of the booths bilge-gray. There were two old, chipped, porcelain sinks under a large dirty mirror, both filled with used paper towels and other flotsam. The floor was similarly littered. On the one bare wall were a thousand fingerprints and, scrawled in lipstick, "Norma is a les" and "Norma loves Ann."

From behind a booth door came a voice: "She said her mother gives them beer. She said her mother gets them all the beer they want."

From another booth came an answer: "That's a lot of *duty*. Her mother is so strict she won't let her out of the house."

First voice: "That's what I told him. He was really bitchin.\* I know he's in college but he looks about twenty-four. He thought she was eighteen. I said 'That's because it's dark in here.' He said, 'If I asked her out, would her mother let her go?' I said no. He said, 'I thought so.'"

Second voice: "Wait for me; I'll be right out."

---

\* Bitchin: A short-lived, college freshman word for great, gorgeous, terrific. See also "tough."

I made other trips to Urban's rest rooms—dragged by Gretel—but never as anything but a tourist. Likewise, I never drank water while I was in the school because on one of my study hall outings I happened to stop at a drinking fountain. Without looking, I turned up the spray and bent down to take a sip. When I opened my eyes I found my face an inch from a wad of deflowered bubble gum, and two inches from a pool of cigarette butts. The natives drank fearlessly from the hall fountains every hour between classes. Obviously, they had built-in immunities.

Spanish class was always a circus, and I never knew what to watch first: the acrobats, the clowns, the performing animals, or the ringmaster. Poor Miss Zorri simply couldn't cope with her troupe. Having to teach two different years of a language simultaneously would have been difficult even under the best of circumstances. The presence of a group of rowdies made it impossible.

One day, when all the rings were madly going at once, I couldn't help myself: I burst out laughing. The sound of that deep, nonvirginal guffaw spun the girl in front of me completely around in her desk.

"Was that you?" she asked. I admitted it was. She looked incredulous.

"How old are you?" she demanded.

"Sixteen and a half," I said.

"What grade are you in?"

"Low eleven."

"Gee," she said, squinting at me. "You look older than me, and I'm younger than you."

"How old are you?" I asked, pondering the meaning of her previous statement.

"Fifteen next month," she said.

"What grade are you in?"

"Low ten."

I gave her the warm, tolerant smile of an older girl who knows she cannot be close friends with anyone so young, but understands her. She accepted it. Next to her, the rowdy named Tony was making basketballs out of notebook paper and tossing them at the wastebasket, muttering "Shit!" every time he missed.

"These boys are very destructive," she observed. "We're all going to go nuts by the end of this class." When Miss Zorri asked us to recite an idiom and the rowdies broke into catcalls, wolf whistles, howls, screeches, and hoots, she turned around and smiled at me. "Nuts," she repeated. "We're all going to go nuts."

She was very right, of course. And the sad thing was that there were a number of students in the room who really wanted to learn Spanish. After a time, the earnest members of the class began to grow angry and resentful, and tried on their own to silence the others. When that happened, the period turned into a civil war. Classmate fought classmate with cries of "Will you guys shut up?" and "Who says so?" and "Don't be such a smart aleck" and "Hiss, bang, boom." That failing, the students who cared then turned their anger on Miss Zorri, plotting, on the days she was most ineffectual, to have her overthrown. The little girl in front of me wanted me, as an older person, to go to the authorities and tell on Miss Zorri. "I'll go with you," she offered pleadingly. She couldn't understand how I could remain so passive. I let her down.

And indeed I was having my own troubles in Spanish class, which I'll describe further on, but even without them, the most interesting thing about that class was the boy named Mickey. He was by far the most attractive boy in any of my classes, and by far the most sophisticated dresser I had seen in the school. He was also the most upsetting of the rowdies because he was the smartest of them. He instigated a great percentage of the trouble they

94

caused and was able to get to Miss Zorri better than his buddies because he could toss his easy knowledge of Spanish in her face.

All of this would have added up to a rather common case except for one thing: Mickey was also in my English class and there he was a model student. Early in the first week he had talked out loud while the English teacher, Mr. Fells, was making an announcement. Mr. Fells stopped dead and reprimanded him and Mickey never tried it again. He turned into a Boy Scout. He was the first volunteer to do chores like open and close windows and go to the supply room for books. He raised his hand and volunteered to answer questions, he paid attention, he did his homework. He was some other boy.

English class generally brought out the best in my classmates. They showed definite signs of life in that room. They read when they were told to and responded when called upon. One day they actually made joyful noises about an assignment—when Mr. Fells told them they were going to study Poe. They loved Poe; they had seen all his movies. As Mr. Fells talked about him, they took down each word. "The French think the world and all of him," said Mr. Fells, and the ball-point pens bobbed rapidly at every desk. "Why do you think he wrote such strange stories?" he asked. The class could barely wait for the answer: "Because it's easier to write about morbid things than about happy things, because it is easier to remember morbid moods and terrible ones than happy moods." Even I wrote that down.

"The Fall of the House of Usher" was the first Poe story assigned to the class, and we were told to read it during class time, noting particularly Poe's exotic vocabulary. Mr. Fells asked if anyone in class had any idea why Poe used such big, fancy words, and after a moment a boy

95

raised his hand to answer. "To make his stories longer," said the boy. I thought that was very incisive of him.

After we read "Usher" we had a spelling-vocabulary quiz on it. Mr. Fells dictated fifteen words which we were to write down and use in a sentence. The words were: domain, annihilate, unobtrusive, orthodox, collateral, patrimony, tarn, inconsistency, accosted, profuse, tremulous, abeyance, palpable, phantasmagoric, and manifest.

We were given a reasonable time to take the quiz and then were told to correct our own papers. Mr. Fells called on pupils at random to spell and define, and, on the whole, the class did well. I probably could have trusted myself to misspell a proper number of the words, but just in case, I spelled inconsistency "inconsistancy." And, well, to be honest, I didn't know what tarn meant. I picked up a way to disguise that fact from my classmates. When they didn't know what a word meant, they would form a sentence that said "I don't know what tarn means" or "Poe uses the word tarn a lot."

The spelling errors they made were easy for an old English major like myself to understand: one *l* in collateral, a middle *a* in patrimony, a middle *a* in orthodox. The student who did the best in both spelling and defining was the boy named Mickey.

It was a great tribute to Mr. Fells, I believe, that he was able to hold the attention of a class with such a diversity of types in it. Every kind of teenager ever grown was in that class: the Boy Wonder who made the honor roll, was elected to class office, and in his spare time was the hope of the tennis team; the earnest, obedient, plain girl who inevitably became teacher's helper; the untouchables who did everything they were supposed to but never got emotionally involved; the swingers; the troublemakers; the followers; the confused; the potential dropouts.

All kinds of chatter fringed the hour. "I hate my

mother," said a girl matter-of-factly as she entered the room. "Me, too," said a girl with her.

"Where's the action?"—I really heard a boy ask it of another.

"At Kevin's."

"Who's gonna be there?" (That follows as the night the day.)

"Sal and Porky, John-o and Shirley, Alf and Barb, George, Kay, Sherm, Gerry, Walt, Tink, and, um, Pete Meyers."

"Is Gerry a boy or a girl?" wound up First Boy.

A girl behind me whispered to the boy next to her, "How old are you now?"

"Nineteen," he answered.

"You'll be twenty when you graduate," she said without emotion.

"Yeah," he said as blandly.

"How's your brother?" he asked her.

"Up in Juvenile," she replied. "Stole a couple of cars."

He grunted.

She said, "Well, what can you do?"

He said, "Yeah."

And there was Mr. Fells, fighting their reveries with references to television and movies and other events they could comprehend. His only trouble areas were politics and personal philosophies—he got them mixed, and inserted both more often than he should have. When he stayed away from them he was fine. Like many of my teachers, he did considerable musing out loud, but unlike most of them, when he finally had his thoughts in order, he made a point and could usually get it across. And that was no small feat, considering the competition he was getting from the noise of first lunch hour outside and the imminence of second lunch hour inside.

"Does anybody here remember a senator from Wisconsin named McCarthy?" he inquired one day in an effort to make a point about "The Lottery." Mickey said he thought he knew the name but didn't know why. No one else in class said a word.

Mr. Fells looked frustrated. "Maybe it was before your time," he said, primarily to himself. Then, forcefully: "There was this senator from Wisconsin, you see, and he . . ."

But he was too late. It was three minutes to lunch. And one, two, three: open purses, grope inside, take out mirrors, combs, compacts, lipsticks.

Comb hair, powder noses, apply lipstick . . . one, two, three, and there goes the bell. SCRAMBLE.

Joseph McCarthy died when my classmates were approximately nine years old. Now in their sixteenth year, when they were about to get the word on McCarthyism from their English teacher, it was time for lunch.

That's the way English class always ended: with a stampede toward the door that ground the mornings underfoot, leaving no trace of them. Then the afternoons sprouted out of the rubble, bringing, for me, lunch hour, gym class, and speech, all of which were so consistently fraught with one thing or another that I'll cover them, later, one at a time.

# 10

THOUGH my teenage world was quickly rounding, something vital was missing from it. In a word: Boys. I had not met any. The reasons, I believe, were that one, I didn't want to; and two, I didn't know how to. It was one thing to communicate with sixteen-year-old girls; quite another, I felt, to communicate with sixteen-year-old boys.

I suppose if I really got self-analytical, I'd find some awfully interesting complications of these reasons in the dark corners of my mind—one of them, perhaps, a fear that I might find myself genuinely attracted to a teenage boy. In my early research for this book, while stalking teenagers through their haunts in the suburbs, I had seen a few really sexy-looking male specimens around swimming pools and tennis courts. I had scared myself even looking at them. I was neither old enough nor young enough to lust after minors. Frank's ominous "Are you going to let them paw you?"—coupled with my friends' fear that I would seduce their son—had likewise scared me.

I was therefore terribly relieved to find that the boys at Urban honestly did not appeal to me. They were too badly groomed and too scrawny. Even the best-looking of them were not put together as well as the majority of the girls. They were years behind their female counterparts in the kind of poise and self-assessment it takes to look attractive. Whereas in the last seventeen years girls have evolved more and more close to physical perfection in their early teens, boys have evolved with longer frames over which is stretched the same amount of flesh the old frames used to hold. What I mean is, the average teenage girl these days looks like a young goddess. The average teenage boy looks like a baby bird in a King Kong costume.

Perhaps, however, I am not qualified to judge the attractions of teenage boys. Inevitably, the boys I thought were least appealing—gawkiest, sloppiest—were constantly ringed by girls. What the boys wore made no difference whatsoever to the girls unless their clothes added up to an obvious badge of character the way black jackets and boots meant Big Trouble. The tidiest outfit worn by boys around school was white jeans, clean shirt, and sneakers. Second tidiest, because by day's end the outfit was showing signs of fatigue, was slacks, shirt, V-neck sweater, and shoes which were not too scuffed, kicked and battered.

Bess was quite concerned about my attitude toward the boys. Whenever she drove me to school (most mornings I took buses) she would slow down at every bus stop and stare out the window. "There's a cute boy," she would say. "And there's a cute one. How about *him*? Why don't you find out who he is? He'd be nice for you; not too tall."

She'd ask me when I got home, too, "Did you meet any boys today?" I'd have to say no, feeling more like a failure every time. And indeed I did think it odd that neither Gretel nor any of the rest of the gang ever introduced me to boys. "Did you try to meet any on your own?" Bess would ask. I had to admit I had not tried. I had, in fact,

100

done just the opposite. One day at lunch a boy had tapped me on the shoulder and I damn near fainted. He came up behind me while I was standing with the gang, and I whirled around as though a cougar had dropped in my trail.

"Hey, somebody over here wants to talk to you," he said. I cautiously lifted my eyes and he pointed to the person who had dispatched him. It was one of the rowdies from Spanish class: Tony the Troublemaker. He was standing with several of the other rowdies, and when I looked at him they all laughed and gave him a couple of shoves. It was a situation so pregnant with possibilities that I panicked. I turned on my heel, grabbed Gretel's arm, and said, "Let's go stand by *that* pillar."

Did I leave behind me the greatest story ever told? I'll never know. I can't believe Tony really wanted to meet me. I think he was putting me on. I was such a strange-looking thing, with all that hair and those glasses and my old face. He had to be kidding. Worse yet, he might not have been kidding. Then what would I have done? ("Dear Frank," I penciled into my notebook. "Today a boy wanted to talk to me but do not worry, my love, he was not clean." Signed "Penelope.")

So Bess decided to take action. "Listen," she said, one afternoon at four as I limped in the door, exhausted as usual from my hard day in the classroom. "I decided that you need help. I hope you don't mind; there was no way I could reach you to check. I called a close friend who has a son about your age—I mean he's a junior in high school. I told her what you're doing and asked her to bring him here for a consultation. He's a wonderful, adorable boy. His name is David Walter Elliot Bodine. He's only fifteen and a half but you'd never know it. He's terribly bright. I'm sure he'll be a big help. He'll be here after dinner. You'll love him."

"I don't want to love him," I said, dropping into a chair.

"You know what I mean," said Bess. "What's the matter with you? You have to meet boys. Otherwise your research will be incomplete."

"It won't help my research to meet a boy you've procured for me," I said. "He'll be uncomfortable with me. I've got to meet boys who don't know how old I am."

"That's the point," she said. "David will introduce you to his friends. He'll be a shortcut."

"You mean he'll be a conspirator," I said.

She nodded.

"What if he doesn't want to? What if he tells everybody in town what I'm doing?"

"He won't," she said. "I don't *think* he will. That's a chance we'll have to take. Now come on, straighten up and don't look so glum. Have your vodka and do your homework and stop brooding. And change your clothes. You look silly in that jumper. Put on your jeans. Take off those glasses and comb those bangs out of your eyes. Look cute, will you?"

I said I'd do my best.

David's mother, Harriet, arrived first. I assumed she'd come to look me over before letting her son get involved, but I was wrong. She had not meant to come alone. She had gone to David's school to pick him up after a club meeting, but had not been able to find him. She was shaking from head to toe and wringing her hands and talking so fast no one could get half her words. She was a wreck. David was not at the appointed meeting place. He had disappeared. His meeting was over and he was nowhere to be found. No one had seen him leave the school grounds. No one knew where he was.

Bess tried to calm her friend, but she just kept chattering. David had never done that before. He was a very good boy. He was always where he was supposed to be.

102

He wouldn't leave if he knew she was picking him up. He knew he had to be at Bess's house. He could only have met with violence.

Harriet called her husband and he drove at once to her side. He sat for a moment going over all the possibilities and then declared, "We must call the police. We mustn't panic. We must call the police and they will find him right away. Now, what's the phone number for the police?"

Enter David. When he rang the doorbell, his parents jumped to their feet and screamed, "They've found him! Thank God, they've found him!" When he came through the door, they landed on him like falling rocks. "Where *were* you?" they shouted.

David looked surprised. He shrugged and shuffled into the living room. "Hermie brought me over," he said. "What's the big deal?" He looked at the floor, moving his jacket zipper up three inches and down two, then up two and down three. He shifted his weight from one foot to another like a boxer in training. "Hi, Mrs. Arthur," he mumbled to Bess. He didn't look at me. I introduced myself with a "Hi, David," and he nodded in my direction and said "Hi."

Yes, David was adorable. He was about five feet eight, maybe one hundred and twenty pounds, maybe less. About four feet one of him was legs; about sixty pounds was his zippered jacket. He had a delicate face with big eyes, and brown curly hair.

He was extremely wary of me. I gave him about a half hour to unwind in the company of Bess and his parents, and then I asked him if he would come into the library for a private discussion.

"Do you mind if I come along?" his father inquired, rising from his chair. He smiled. "Unless you two have to be alone," he said. He came along.

103

"You know about my going to high school here, don't you?" I asked David, as soon as we settled down.

He nodded.

"What do you think about it?"

"It's illegal, isn't it?" he said. Then, little by little, he indicated that he didn't like what I was doing at all. He was very loyal to the local high schools. He thought they were the best in the state. He was upset because I was getting away with passing. He felt I was making fools of teachers, and teachers meant a great deal to him. There was something else in his attitude, something even more subtle: he was embarrassed by the thought that an adult should be in on all the nuances of a school day. "It must look very silly to you," he said without looking at me. And still without looking at me he asked, "Aren't you bored?" Later, he used the word "bored" again, saying, "You must be really bored." And again: "Classes are really boring, don't you think?"

I told him I was rarely bored during the school day. "Tired, yes," I said. "Worn out, absolutely. And yes, I find it hard to pay attention. But I'm not bored."

David wasn't convinced. "I'd be bored in your shoes," he said. What I didn't know at the time was that he used the words "bored" and "boring" as often as the rest of us use a, an, and the. He was one of the "cool" kids, a different cat from my friends at Urban. There were cool kids at Urban, too, I discovered, but they were a very small, special group. Surprisingly, I found them easier to understand than the apparently less complex youngsters in my own gang. But we'll get to that later.

David was not attending Urban even though he lived within its district. He was going to the new high school a few miles from town, which was, in a sense, siphoning off all the best students in the city. His school, he told me, had cost two and a half million dollars to build. It was

104

modern and had the best of everything. It even had a coffee break at ten in the morning, when you could go down to the cafeteria and get juice or milk and cake, and then walk around outside for ten minutes. It was flat, he said, and had huge windows so the sun could come in. It stood on twelve acres of ground that had a great big fountain in the middle. It was really cool, he said.

"How are you going to know about schools like mine?" he asked. "If you just go to one high school, you'll think they're all like that. If you just meet Urban kids, you'll think they're everybody. How are you going to know about the kids at my school?"

"I'll know from you," I said. "That's what you can do—help me get a better picture of what's going on."

I told him I understood his suspicions of me. "I know I'm not meeting all the teenagers in America," I said. "I know there are all kinds." I tried, as best I could, to make him understand that I wanted to do an honest reporting job, and that it was because I did want to set the record straight that I had chosen what he considered an "illegal" method to get my story.

David had a marvelously mature, cynical smile. And he sat across from me on a desk chair smiling very slowly, very cynically. He asked me if I would ever tell what city I had been in. I said I would not. He nodded his head.

Silence.

"What are you going to do about getting picked up?" he asked.

"Picked up?"

"Yeah, you know. Guys will try to pick you up."

"Do you think so?" I asked.

"Sure. Some of the guys around here move very fast."

"I don't know what I'll do," I said. "I'll worry about it when the time comes."

Then came a voice from the corner. "Keep it above the waist, above the waist," it said. I had forgotten David's

105

father was in the room. We looked at him suddenly and he laughed. "Just keep it above the waist," he said again.

David blushed. So did I. We changed the subject.

David said he had a heavy schedule and was worried about getting into college. He had begun cramming for his College Boards. He thought my schedule was ridiculous, and felt I should at least be taking plane geometry.

"I'd flunk plane geometry," I said.

"No you wouldn't," he said. "I'd help you with it."

"Would you really?" I asked. "If you would, maybe I'll switch one of my courses and take geometry."

"Sure," he said. "I've got some extra time after school. I'll come over or you can call me up. And listen, let me tell you something. You should smile more. You look scared to death. Nobody's going to talk to you if you look like that. You look much younger when you smile."

I thanked him, and looked at the floor. I decided it was not the time to ask him to fix me up with his friends. I'd wait.

"Listen, what do you think of these glasses?" I asked.

David winced. "Do you have to wear them?"

"They hide these lines, don't you think?"

"Yeah, I guess they do," he said.

His father stood up, rubbed his hands together, slapped David on the back, and announced that he thought it was okay to leave us alone for a while.

As soon as he left, David turned to me. "Listen," he whispered, "I know Bess told you I'm not really sixteen. Nobody knows it around here. I don't want them to. So you don't tell how old I am, and I won't tell how old you are. Okay?"

We shook hands on it.

Once upon a time I loved a boy who looked like David. I remembered him as soon as David went home. A boy named Billy who didn't love me in return. When I was fifteen and Billy was sixteen, I thought he looked just like Tyrone Power. My mother couldn't see it. She thought he looked like a cute little boy with a bad complexion.

I loved Billy all through my teens. He was my life force—the why and wherefore, the beginning and the end. Billy was also the only reason I ever got any exercise. I pedaled my bicycle past His House. Around the block, past His House. Up the street, past His House. Down the hill, around the corner, over the river and past His House. Did he see me? Did I see him? Later on I exchanged my bike for a car and drove past His House. Gas rationing was over. The gear shift was on the steering wheel. I never went boy hunting without having to shift gears. By the time hydromatic drive came along, the thrill of the hunt was gone. No, that wasn't it, the hunted were gone: gone to college, gone to work in a summer job, real gone. By the time gears shifted automatically, you brought boys home with you on vacations.

Young David made me remember it all. . . .

"I saw Billy today."

"Gee, you did? Did he see you?"

"I don't know for sure. I think so. But I don't know for sure if he was home; his bike wasn't there. But the window was open in his room, so I'm not sure. And Tom was home because I went past his house and his bike/car was there, but Billy's wasn't so maybe he was in the back yard and was just going into his house when I went by, but I didn't turn around to look in case he was there."

And more:

"I think I saw Billy today."

"Gee, you did? Where?"

"I think he rode past my house. I'm not sure, it might have been Tom because he has a blue car/bike, too. It went so fast I couldn't tell if it was the Blue Dragon or the Blue Cat. I know it wasn't the Green Hornet though."

And more:

107

"Hey, that's them, I think."

"Where?"

"At the stop sign. Hurry. C'mon, they're coming."

"Oh, I think it is. Oh nuts, they're leaving. Was that the black Olds?"

"Yes. Sure it was. I saw it right there."

"Well, then, it must've been. Who else could it be? It was the Black Maria. Oh golly. Do you think they saw us?"

"I don't know, but they saw the house."

"Oh, go call Smitty. Tell her. Ask her if she can come over because maybe they'll come back. And tell her to hurry. Was that Billy in the front?"

"I don't know for sure, but who else could it be? Because Spongy and Billy were going to basketball practice, remember? And they had to pick up Alan afterward."

"Gee, that's right. Then I'll bet it *was* Billy. And why did they go up Walnut Street if they didn't want to see us? Go call Smitty."

"Hi, Smitty."

"Hi" is the magic word. Hi, Gretel. Hi, David.

"Hi, David."

About ten-thirty of the night I met David, the phone rang and Bess answered it. "It's for you," she said, smiling. "It's David."

"Hi, David," I said.

"Hi," he answered. "Listen, I was thinking. Maybe you'd like to go to the football game with me next Friday night. It's the first this year. We play East City and it'll probably be a bore, but they're going to leave the school open before the game and you can see what it looks like. If you can go, I mean."

"Sure, David, I can go," I said. "I'd like to very much. It's very nice of you to ask me. What do I wear to a night football game?"

He giggled. "I don't know what girls wear," he said. "I guess you wear whatever girls wear. A skirt and a sweater, something like that. Whatever you wear to school."

"Okay, fine. What time?"

"I don't know. I'll have to call you after school Friday. Listen, can you get a car?"

"A car? Gee, I don't know. I'll have to ask Bess. I haven't driven out here because I can't carry my license. I don't know my way around at all."

"That's okay. I'll direct you. But I can't drive till February seventeenth. It would help if you could drive because otherwise my dad'll have to pick us up."

"Okay, I'll try," I said.

"Okay," he said. "I'll call you. So long."

Bess did a short, delighted jig when I hung up. "Hooray," she said. "You've got a date. Now we'll see some action around here. Aren't you excited? What a riot. I can't wait until Friday."

"Me either," I said. Which wasn't exactly accurate. I knew I could wait until Friday night. I just didn't know if I could survive.

# 11

THE INTERESTED, it is said, can determine the exact age of a tree by counting the rings in its trunk. In order to do so, of course, they first have to saw it down. Since my days at Urban, I've begun to wonder if the same might not be true for women—that the only way to determine how old they are is to saw them in half. I think that's what's going on in those police laboratories where they identify corpses; they're counting rings. And even so, you'll notice, medical examiners rarely commit themselves on anything but an approximate figure. You never read in newspapers that the thing in the ditch was a woman *exactly* twenty-eight years old. The report always says *about* twenty-eight, or between twenty-six and, say, thirty-four.

Perhaps you think any doctor could tell you the age of a live woman, just by examining her. I certainly would have thought so. But let me tell you about the curious incident that took place the morning after I met young David Bodine.

It was about 10:15 A.M. and study hall was peacefully under way. The girl with the bobbin hair had already come and gone, and since nothing ever happened in study hall, no more interruptions were anticipated. Like the rest of the class, I was doing some homework I should have done the night before—memorizing Spanish verbs, in this case. At a moment when the room was particularly quiet, the door swung open and in strode a tall, solid, blond girl who looked like either a Phys Ed lieutenant or a knight errant. Everyone in the room quickly lifted his head—the kids always do that when someone walks into class, jerk up like deer at a water hole getting a new scent—and waited, vacantly, for something interesting to happen.

The girl handed a piece of paper to the teacher and then stood back with her arms locked across her chest. He read the note, set it down, put on his glasses, and looked around the room. Something about the way he was passing his eyes up and down the rows troubled me. The rest of the class went back to reading. I stayed alert.

The teacher picked up the note again. "Tornabene?" he thundered (or so it seemed). "Is there a Tornabene in here?"

I raised my hand.

The teacher shrugged. "I don't even know you, Tornabene," said. "You're wanted."

I felt as if I'd been kicked in the head. Surely I had been expecting to hear those words, but I don't know . . . not this particular morning. Everything was going so well. The addition of David to my life had rounded out everything so perfectly. The morning had started so brightly and full of promise. I even looked better, I thought. I had on a new blouse Bess had brought home for me which was typical of Urban attire, and I felt quite safely camouflaged. My morale had risen appreciably; I had even held my head up in home room. I didn't want to be discovered; not this morning.

111

I got out of the desk, straightened, and moved stiffly forward.

"No. Take your books," the teacher instructed.

I sat down again and gathered my belongings out of the rack by my side, dropping papers as I did so, and stuffing them loosely into my notebook. I tried not to panic. I tried to think clearly about what I was going to say and how I would say it. There was no reason to be so wildly scared, I told myself. What could they do to me? Maybe they'd be amused. Maybe they'd let me disappear without exposing me publicly—without Gretel and the other kids having to know. Maybe they'd even let me stay in school.

All of this rushed through my mind as I tried to slow my pulse and breathe normally. But there was something uncontrollable about my feelings. Though my fear was unreasonable, it had a life of its own. I was no more prepared to be taken to the principal's office at the age of thirty-three and eleven twelfths than I had been at seven.

I joined the lieutenant at the door and fell into step behind her. She didn't say a word.

"Where are we going?" I asked.

"To the nurse's office," she said without turning.

"The nurse's office?" I exclaimed to the back of her head.

"Yes. The nurse's office."

I ran a little to reach her side and, when I got there, tugged at her sweater sleeve to make her stop. She didn't. "But I'm not sick," I said, by now skipping.

Abruptly she stopped and looked at me disdainfully. "All new students have to have physicals," she announced, emphasizing every syllable as though she were addressing a dolt.

"I had a physical at the school I just left," I lied.

She shook her head in despair of my stupidity. "Well,

you have to have one here, too, so just hurry up and stop stalling."

When she left me in the nurse's office, I felt slightly relieved. At least it wasn't the principal's office. It wasn't the worst that could happen. But good God, then I looked around the room at the scale and the eye chart and the cubbyhole that had a sign DR. EMERY on it—and it fell on me: this was worse than the worst. It was *impossible*. I simply could not have a physical.

Furthermore, there was a whole scene of normal high school insanity going on around me, and I thought, This is a theater of the absurd, it couldn't be anything else. There was a girl waiting with me, also for a physical. She was a combination of Tuesday Weld and Sue Lyon plus a couple of old European sex kittens and all the new pussy-cats of the world. Blond, of course. Five feet four inches tall and one hundred and ten round pounds (I can be so specific because I took notes when she was weighed and measured) neatly wrapped in a sleeveless pink turtleneck stretch top and matching skirt. Like magic, word of her presence carried through the air to every boy in the area, and before you could say hi the room was alive with strapping young fellows complaining of headaches, fevers, and muscular aches and pains. The nurse sent all but two of them back to class clutching aspirin; the others she told to lie down on the cots in the sickroom and keep quiet. As soon as the nurse turned her back, they hopped off the cots and stood at the door making time with the pussycat.

"Oh, you guys are *awful*. You're *terrible*. You're *perverted*," she giggled as they suggested she join them in the sickroom.

Meanwhile I tried to stay calm and fill out forms about my childhood diseases. But then the pussycat, who was ahead of me alphabetically, went to a chair by the win-

113

dow to have her eyes tested and—ugh—it fell on me again.

*I can not have my eyes tested. I have an astigmatism. I am wearing fake eyeglasses. I will not be able to read the eye chart any better with my glasses on than with them off. The nurse will ask me what kind of glasses I am wearing. She will look through them. She will FIND OUT.*

You won't believe the rest of this, but it's true, I swear. The nurse sat me down in front of the chart, saying, "First we'll test your eyes with your glasses, then without them. Okay?" She smiled and walked a few steps behind me. I looked up at the chart. It wasn't the chart, it was a reflection of it in a mirror. The real chart was reversed right behind my head. That prevents cheating. I squinted both eyes and stared at the mirrored letters I was supposed to read. I saw a big E.

"Cover your right eye, please," said the nurse.

And just then a boy walked in and bellowed from the counter that he needed an aspirin.

"Can't it wait?" asked the nurse.

"No," said the boy, who happened to be wearing a cable-stitched sweater with a football letter on it.

"I'll be right back," the nurse said to me, and she flitted through the door to the medicine pantry. Within a split second all my criminal instincts bubbled to the surface. I pivoted around, read the 20/20 line backwards and memorized it. When the nurse returned and asked me to read it aloud, I did so letter-perfectly, one eye at a time.

"Now without your glasses, please," she said, and I read it normally.

"That's fine," she said. "Thank you."

By the time Dr. Emery was ready to see me I was a babbling idiot. Dr. Emery turned out to be Ethel Emery, a pretty lady in her late thirties, wearing a smock, a

114

frown, and eyeglasses. She told me to take off my skirt and blouse and sit in the chair near her desk, and I did, mindlessly. No, not mindlessly. I was totally, heatedly, aware of every square inch of my skin and each individual layer of fat under it. My flabby upper arms had turned into a pair of elephant ears, flapping in the wind.

I sat before her desk in my bra and half-slip while she went over my medical history.

"Are you taking any regular medication?" she asked.

I nodded. "Hormone pills."

"Hormone pills?"

"Yes. A doctor gave them to me for, er, cramps. You see, I have this trouble once in a while, and he gave me hormone pills. When I left home he said maybe I shouldn't take them anymore because . . . um . . . they're, ah, making me grow, you know, a little fast. And, well, I left before I could see him. And I haven't been feeling too well. I guess I'm nervous. And also my throat hurts today." (Note: it did.)

"Um," said Dr. Emery. "I see." She walked over to me. "Say ah."

"Ahhhhhhh."

She looked in my mouth and down my sore throat. I wondered if she'd be blinded by my four gold inlays.

"Nothing wrong here," she said.

She peered into my eyes, ears, and nose. She took my blood pressure. She listened to my heartbeat through an icy stethoscope. She tapped my crossed knee with a gavel. She looked through my hair for cooties. Then she made some notes, and glanced at me indifferently.

"You're fine," she said. "You can get dressed now."

When I walked out of that room a free woman, there was not a doubt in my mind that the whole world was crazy. Or blind. Or overdosed with strontium 90. The next day, when I woke up with a rampaging cold which extended upward from my cleavage to my eyebrows, I considered the possibility that Ethel Emery was just a lousy doctor.

But I don't know. Maybe she was playing it cool. Or maybe she was recording me for medical history.

116

# 12

——————

Fifty minutes a go-go. That's what lunch hours were. More than any other time in the day, the week, or the life of Urban teenagers. Lunch hours were what go-going was all about. Lunch hours explained go-go—in pace, in sound, in feel—the whole jumpy, zingy, nervous, itchy, finger-snapping, where-the-action-is twitch of youth that never had a real definition until the French said *go-go*. Get off the ground. Go, man, go. Go, Rocket Baby, go. *Au go-go. À la go-go. Aux go-go.* To the go-go; at the go-go; in the go-go; on the go-go; by the go-go; for the go-go. Boy meets girl *au go-go.*

Lunch hours at Urban High. For me, the hours I got to know Gretel and the gang. Got to dig them. Got the message. Got the sound. More so in those successive fifty-minute hours than at any other time.

The overture was the stamping and shuffling of a thousand feet and the slamming of a thousand metal locker doors.

"Hey, why don't you put your books in *my* locker?" Gretel offered on typical lunch hour. I still had no locker of my own and had been going to the cafeteria every day loaded down like a pack mule.

"Here, I'll give you the combination, but don't give it to *anybody*. We're not allowed to share lockers. So don't tell *anybody*. Come on, I'll show you how to open it and then you'll be able to use it whenever you want to."

She turned the lock: right, 12; left, all the way around 0 to 54; right, all the way around to 8; back to 50. The narrow steel green door swung open, freeing, as it did so, a pile of books topped by a fuzzy yellow sweater. All spilled on the floor, leaving behind a mountain of other books, notebooks, and sweaters.

"Are those all *yours?*" I asked in genuine astonishment.

"Oh no," said Gretel. "A couple of other kids have the combination, too. Let's see. Tipsy does, and Caroline. And Ellen. And Boo. And a girl in history class, I forget her name, and Miriam. And, oh, I don't know, a couple of others. But there's room for your stuff. Here, give me your notebook. I'll put that in first here in the back, and then we'll put your other stuff down the sides."

"Just take the books and my sweater, I'll hold my notebook," I said. (That notebook could get me hanged, and I was considering chaining it to my wrist.)

And by God, somehow she managed to stow all of my junk, plus all that had fallen on the floor, into the already glutted locker space. She slammed the door on the whole heaving mess, flipped the lock, and we marched off to the cafeteria.

Urban's cafeteria was not big enough to accommodate even a third of the student body. For sheer bedlam, it simply defied competition. There were just too many bodies trying to fit into its inadequate space, but all the same, there they were, like the books and sweaters in Gretel's locker. Many kids stood all through lunch, half eating and half table-hopping and wholly making themselves heard. There was only one way to sit down to eat and that was to purloin a stool. Sometimes even that didn't work. One day Gretel and I stole a couple of stools somebody had hidden under a table, hid them under another table while we stood on the hot line, and found them stolen when we returned. Billy was able to offer one stool she held with her left leg ("Here," she said, flipping it at me, "put your ass on this"), but Gretel ate her lunch that day crouching next to Roxanne.

The same groups assembled at the same tables every day. Sophomores grouped up near the hot food section, good kids to the right, troublemakers to the left. Juniors sat way back near the wall, center and right; seniors center and left. The types referred to as "bad news" formed a gauntlet near the counters holding the only palatable food in the place: hot dogs, sandwiches, and ice cream. In order to procure any of those goodies you had to run the gauntlet and some days it really wasn't worth it. Every time I went for a hot dog I had severe physical encounters with at least three hostiles, and I always had the feeling I was in on the grab for the last morsel of food on earth.

The kids themselves did not find the cafeteria disturbing. They had long ago adjusted to both its conditions and its food. Which should prove, once again, how flexible is the human animal.

My own group ranked high in the junior class pecking order. Only Georgia Katz's gang had more prestige. Georgia's crew was more affluent and more scholarly, though I use the latter word loosely because Urban was not noted for scholastic achievement. My gang stood out among average kids, even though it was average itself. Oddly enough, I could not determine who its leader was. Gretel? Billy? Probably one of the two.

Lunch hours quickly took on a specific shape that barely altered from day to day. Always they began with a search for seats, a struggle to secure food, and then a

119

settling in on our turf. Avis could be counted upon to perch near the table with at least two new copies of Beatle bulletins announcing that the Beatles had risen and set, flowed and ebbed, God's in his heaven, all's right with the world. The gang would frantically catch up with the morning's news and scan the cafeteria. The day's Hot Topic might be the waist-length fake pigtail attached to the head of a friend of Georgia's and everybody would agree how ghastly it looked and appoint Billy to find out where she had bought it and for how much. Then there'd be talk about our own clothes and hairdos.

It was hard to determine who owned what kind of clothes in the gang because there was so much lending and borrowing going on. One day Kelly would be wearing the blazer jacket I was used to seeing on Billy, another day Roxanne would have on Gretel's favorite sweater—or maybe it was Roxanne's sweater and Gretel had borrowed it. No matter. Everything personal was communal: lipsticks, combs, eyeglasses, cigarettes.

Cigarettes. That was the loaned and borrowed item that got to me. There was a considerable amount of smoking done in the johns at lunch, usually by at least eight girls with two cigarettes among them. Only once did I venture to the lav with Gretel "for a stake" and that was my limit partially because I didn't care to get expelled for smoking illegally, and partially because I was too old for the ordeal. I didn't want to puff on a cigarette that was being handed from unknown girl to unknown girl (or even known girl to known girl), and I didn't want to breathe the smoke that hung in the bathroom like smog on a Los Angeles freeway.

Usually Gretel and I were the last ones at our table. We arrived late and ate comparatively slowly. Our gang regularly swallowed their lunches in about eight minutes and ran outside to play, leaving Gretel and me to have serious discussions. During these I picked up incidental information. For instance, there were a lot of lesbians around, Gretel said, and a lot of queers. She didn't say around where and I didn't ask her because I was trying to remember if I had talked so knowingly about homosexuality at her age. I couldn't remember that I had or that any of my friends had.

She told me nobody dug folk music in this town, but she liked it. She guessed that I liked it, too. I looked to her like the type who liked folk singing, she said, and she was willing to bet I spent a lot of Sundays in Greenwich Village with folk hippies. Actually, she admitted, she thought the kids with the long hair and the guitars were pretty silly. "You know," she said, "everybody says beatniks are trying to be different and they're nonconformists and everything, but they're not. They all wear the same clothes and that long hair and do everything alike."

During one of our intimate luncheon discussions, I told her, in answer to her questions, the fictional story of how and why I happened to be at Urban.

She listened quietly. When I'd finished, she patted my hand. "Don't worry," she said. "It will all work out fine. Your mother will remarry and then you'll go and live with her and your stepfather, and everything will be fine. You'll see."

That, Gretel said, was what had happened to her. Why, she had lived in about seven places until her mother remarried: with relatives who didn't understand her ("Okies from New England"), in boarding schools, with friends. She had been in and out of six schools in four years. She had been lonely and scared and thought she'd never have a home anywhere. But see how wrong she was? Now she had a stepfather and a house and lots of clothes, and everything was fine.

Life was good, she insisted. You have to keep happy,

she told me, and have fun, and not worry about things. The only thing that upset her, "to be honest," was the break with her steady. He had done the breaking because he thought they were getting too serious. He wanted to go to college, he didn't want to be involved. Gretel had sort of thought she might marry him and all, and boy, she was lucky to be out of *that* because look how *mean* he had turned out to be.

She wanted to be a dress designer when she got out of school. She hadn't told anybody and I shouldn't either, but she'd been sending sketches to a place in New York that was going to tell her if she had any talent. If I was interested, she'd tell me where it was; she'd found it advertised in some magazine. She wanted to go to New York when she graduated from Urban. She'd never get into college, she said, with all her crazy marks at all those schools, so why pretend? She wanted an apartment of her own, furnished the way she wanted it. Even if it was ugly. Maybe just pillows on the floor, great big fat pillows. If it could just be hers and not have modern furniture in it.

But she hated to get so *serious*. And she hated me to worry about anything. "Golly, you look so *sad*. You should see how silly you look. Now, come on, stop that. Everything's going to be fine. Cooky's mother got married last year, too, even, so you see, everybody does. Honest. Everything is going to be fine. You just feel bad now, but you'll see. . . . Come on. Let's go to the john for a drag. You have any Kents? Come on, we'll find some. Then we'll go outside and see everybody."

And outside, it was like this:

Gretel: "Hey, Lyn, let's go over and talk to Janey."

"Okay."

Roxanne: "Oh, there's Gina over there near the other side of the wall. Let's all go talk to her."

"Okay."

Kelly: "Hey, who's Arlene talking to? Julieanne. Boy, she looks bad news. Let's go talk to her."

Billy: "Hey, Gretel. C'mere a minute. C'mere, you guys."

Gretel: "Let's go stand over there in the sun."

"That's a good idea. Let's."

Roxanne: "There's too much sun over here. Let's go over there."

"Okay."

Kelly: "Ohhhh. Tipsy's got a radio. Let's go stand with Tipsy. Let's sing: If I trust innn you, da da dadadada."

Let's go in. Let's go out. Let's stand here. Let's sit down. Let's move these coats. Let's get our sweaters. Let's buy some football tickets. Let's look at the bus.

And the purpose of it all—every jerky, twitchy, yo-yo, hot-foot move—was to be in the best possible spot to see and be seen by (what else?) boys.

Little did I dream that I had stumbled upon a serious mating season. I mean, teenage girls are always looking for guys. But what was going on during lunch in the opening weeks of school amounted to hysteria. It was post-summer-breakup, pre-who-are-you-going-with? time.

*Everybody* broke up at the end of summer; that fact had been impressed on me at once. So September was roundup time, branding time, reshuffle time, fill-the-vacuum time. In later months, life would settle into who belongs to whom, and the mating game would be more subtle. The Thing in September was to get a guy *now*, because without one a girl was nobody all year.

Every contact with a boy was serious, though you might not know that without a script. Take, for instance, my own first experience with the game. I had left the cafeteria with Gretel and walked with her to the spot where our gang was jumping up and down in space. Among the usual group members was the girl named

Tipsy, a lively little dark-haired pixie, with a boy from English class, tall, gawky, long-haired, and pleasant-faced.

Tipsy, her miniature transistor radio held tightly to her right ear, was mildly frugging to a tune only she could hear. "Oh, Kelly," she said, rolling her head in a one-two beat, "I had a dream about George Harrison." (That's a Beatle.) "It was so *sharp*. It was so *real*. I dreamt George held my hand!"

"Oh, Tipsy, how *tough!*" exclaimed Kelly, envy curdling her pitch.

"Oh, it was, it was," said Tipsy, frugging stronger now, and humming a bit of the tune filtering into her right ear. "Da da dee da dummm . . . until my mother came in and said 'Wake up, wake up.' But it was such a *tough* dream . . . dum da dum dee."

"Tipsy, you're nuts," said the boy.

"No, you're *crazy*," said Tipsy.

Everyone giggled.

Then somehow the subject of topless bathing suits came up and the boy said he was going to buy a *bottom*less bathing suit and Billy said he should wear two walnuts and a fig leaf. That, of course, brought on more giggles, as well as much shuffling of feet and playful jabbings.

Gretel, during this exchange, had not said a word. Later, as we went off to gym class, she whispered to me, "Did you see that boy?"

I nodded.

"I like him," she said.

If she hadn't told me, I never would have known.

The boy-girl game as played by Roxanne and Kelly had me completely confused. When I was doing research for this book, a fifteen-and-a-half-year-old cosmopolite told me that girls who were crazy for the Beatles were girls who had no real boyfriends. I tested this thought on other high school girls and found them in agreement with it. Later I read it, expanded upon, in articles by child experts. I accepted it. It made sense to me, and I filed it in my mind as a working fact. The only trouble was, it didn't hold up in the face of two genuine Beatle nuts like Roxanne and Kelly. They were as far gone as girls could go over that historic quartet, but they also liked real boys. Roxanne, in particular, was very flirtatious, but no grass grew under the black-stockinged, booted feet of either.

To a matron disguised as a teenager, R and K were an endless puzzle. They had two distinct approaches to conversation. One was high-pitched, silly, and Beatle-oriented. The other was straight, sensible, and adult. More than any other girls I met, they exemplified The Teenager, swinging back and forth, as they did, like open gates in a hurricane, between adolescence and maturity.

One day they kept me company while Gretel and Billy sneaked into the building for a cigarette. After giddily waving good-bye to them and screeching threats to turn them in, they turned to me very soberly and asked, with all the poise in the world, whether I planned to go to college and where. We talked about me and my transfer problems and they were sanely attentive and responsive. Then I asked them if they wanted to go to college, and, almost in unison, they replied that yes, they did, but they weren't sure they'd make it, and anyway, what they wanted to do more was go to England and work in London until they got enough money to go to Liverpool and live where the Beatles used to live. In a veritable avalanche of breathless phrases, Roxanne told me that her father had given her permission to go during the following summer if she earned her own way, and Kelly told me her father had not yet given in, but she was working on him. "*Liverpool*, oh *God*. Can you imagine? We'd die. We'd just die."

Without pausing then, they calmly invited me to go

with them to the football game in the event Gretel couldn't go. They told me where to meet them and directed me to buy a ticket at the booth set up in the courtyard. Very conscientiously they checked my student activities card and my bus pass to see that they were in order, and just as I was about to ask what I should wear, they left me, first mentally, and then physically. Roxanne spotted a guy ("God, there's Scotty") and poked Kelly. Kelly gasped, and, poof, they were gone.

And then, nearly every day at lunch, there was the matter of the search for Gretel's ex. I was glad of it, really, because it gave me a chance to travel. Have you been to a pep rally lately? I have. I dropped in on one during a search. Gretel and I had seen *him* talking to Roxanne by the stone eagle, but while we were maneuvering into a better position, he got away. Gretel figured maybe he was sitting out the rest of lunch hour at the pep rally, and, well, checking out that notion appealed to me anyway, because, frankly, I was always very fond of pep rallies and I hardly get to them anymore.

The action had already started when we got to the auditorium, and we groped and tripped our way down to the first eight rows, where the small but exuberant group of fans was clustered.

There were more people on the stage than in the audience. Under white lights so bright their glare seemed opaque, sat the Urban High band, resplendent in red, brown, and brass. In front of the band were eight female cheerleaders in short short red felt skirts, white shirts and brown vests. They were doing their best to form a line across the stage, but it stretched out so thin they looked like the Rockettes after a plague. They carried giant pompoms, about the size of beach balls, which they used the way strippers use feathers. In front of them were three boy cheerleaders in white pants and sweaters, all three of whom were built like *Harper's Bazaar* cover girls.

While students were still filing into the auditorium, the cheerleaders kept up a steady chant of "Go, go, go-go-go," accompanied by the drummer. Then they began to bounce up and down, going higher with every jump as though the stage floor were a trampoline. The band broke into a local version of "When the Saints Go Marchin' In" and the cheerleaders taunted the audience into singing along. The building shook.

While the vibrations were still palpable, the band switched to an adaptation of "Has Anybody Seen My Gal?" The boy cheerleaders stepped aside, the girls moved forward in a mashed potato step. Then they set down their pom-poms and did the swim, weirdly unbuttoning a vest button with each backstroke. From the audience came stamps and hoots and whistles and shrieks of "Go, go, go-go-go." The band played louder and the girls came on stronger with their striptease motions. Then *boom boom* went the bass drum, and all movement stopped. *Boom.* Like that.

The band stayed quiet, and the cheerleaders, boys and girls, fanned out across the stage. The head cheerleader stepped forward and called for a big "Kill 'em" cheer. I grinned at Gretel but she didn't notice. She was up on her left knee searching the house row by row for you know who.

"BROWN AND RED,
KILL EM DEAD
RIGHT ON THE HEAD
YAY.
WHO'S GONNA WIN?
WE'RE GONNA WIN.
YAAAAAAAY. Yay team, yay team, yay team."

The drummer began pounding again, and every voice in the place stretched and stretched and stretched into a mighty chorus of "Go, go, go-go-go. Go, go, go-go-go."

And the cheerleaders were bouncing and their pompoms were waving and the band was playing and I thought I was going to die of internal hysterics. "I don't believe it," I said to myself. "I don't believe I am sitting here cheering at a pep rally. This is a scene from *Bye Bye Birdie,* and I am being put on as nobody has ever been before." I let myself laugh, just a little, to take the pressure off my ribs. How, I wondered, will I ever be able to share this quarter hour? How?

I looked over at Gretel to see if perhaps she was by now caught up in the screwball excitement. To my surprise, her chair was empty. I turned around just in time to catch sight of her dashing out of the auditorium. Either she had found him or she was still hunting him. *¿Quién sabe?* she was gone.

The drum rolled. The cheerleaders marched forward. The band stood up. "Now *everybody* up," they pleaded, "and let's *hear* it:

> *Urban High, we love you.*
> *You're our school, yes you are.*
> *Whene'er we leave we'll send you*
> *All our hopes from afar."*
> *Go, Urban. GO."*

What *were* we when we were teenagers? Were we Gretel and Cooky and Roxanne and Kelly and all these jazzy, jumpy cats? Would they, someday, be us? Were they us already?

# 13

"WHAT's black and white and gray all over?" . . . "Sister Mary Elephant."

"What do you call the black, oozy stuff between an elephant's feet?" . . . "Slow natives."

These were two of the jokes Cooky and Gretel told me one gym period as we sat killing time in the auditorium. It seemed, for a while, that gym class was established for the sole purpose of exercising the vocal cords. Two weeks ticked by before the gyms were ready for use, and meanwhile I had an hour every day to listen to my friends exchange words. Jokes were an important part of the exchange. Cooky and Gretel could trot out all their old ones because I represented a new audience for them. Usually there were just the three of us trapped together; once in a while we'd be joined by others, who transferred in and out of the hour while they made changes in their schedules.

There were last-gasp elephant jokes, as above, last-gasp fruit jokes, and self-conscious dirty jokes. Samples:

Fruit category: "What's forty feet long, purple, and lives in the ocean?" . . . "Moby Plum."

"What's yellow and goes *zzzzzzz?*" . . . "An electric banana."

Dirty category: "What did the newborn baby say to the doctor?" . . . "Don't hit me so hard; I was made with only one screw."

And another, having to do with a big sister watching her little brother "going wee-wee" in the bathroom, giving him orders like "Attention," and "At ease," and having him respond with his "little penis." The punch line was "Attention, at ease, charge," and Cooky illustrated it with a piece of paper rolled into a phallus. I can't really tell it properly because it was a visual gag.

Between jokes, Gretel told me about how she and Cooky laughed at nothing and anything and silly things, and people heard them and wondered what they were laughing at. I didn't wonder what they were laughing at half as much as I wondered why the sound of their laughter was different from older ladies'. Virginal laughter, I think it is called. But even older ladies who are virgins don't laugh at that pitch. It's indescribable and inimitable and either you have it or you don't. Since I didn't (and don't), I could only smile at their jokes. They howled at them.

Figuring it took five minutes to get settled after gym class got under way, there were then forty-five minutes to fill with conversation. That's a lot, as anyone who's been trapped between two strangers on an airplane can testify. Sometimes the girls ran out of talk and just made sounds. Sometimes they gave themselves up to the boredom that constantly threatened, and let it ravage them. Somehow, the minutes always passed.

During the first day or two, Gretel and Cooky informed me I had to get a gym suit. When they asked, I told them yes, I had my sneakers and socks, but no, my gym suit hadn't arrived yet.

"What kind of gym suit do you wear out here?" I inquired.

130

"Oh, it's *hor*-ribull," said Gretel. "It's some horrible old color blue, and it has bloomers."

"Bloomers!" I exclaimed.

"Yes, honest. Why? What was yours like?"

"Oh, mine was, ah, mine was, was blue, too, but it didn't have bloomers. It had—a skirt. Yes. A skirt with pleats, and you wore kind of shorts under it that matched —were the same color. And, ah, well, we certainly didn't have to wear *bloomers.*"

"Well, you'll wear them here," said Cooky. "You can probably wear shorts for a while, but you better get a gym suit as fast as you can."

"I think I'd like to get some new shoes, too," I said.

Gretel agreed that I needed them. "Your shoes are cute and all, but out here we wear heels, like these." The heels to which she referred were lower than the "baby dolls" which were, upon my fourteenth birthday, my own first pair of "heels."

"They're *cute,*" I said.

"Exactly how old are you?" asked Cooky, my inquisitor. She got my standard reply: "Sixteen and a half."

"Me too," said Gretel. "I *thought* you were my age. When's your birthday?"

"Guess," I suggested, not knowing.

"December?"

"Unh-unh."

"April?"

"Unh-unh."

"February. I'll bet it's February."

"Right! How'd you know?"

"Because that's when *mine* is. What date?"

"Guess."

"Twenty-second?"

"Unh-unh. The thirteenth."

"*Eeeeeee!*" shrieked Gretel. "Right near mine. Mine's

131

the twenty-second. Wouldn't it have been *funny* if yours was the *same?*"

"Gee, yes. But it's almost the same."

"We're almost twins," Gretel said, overcome with joy.

"So what?" asked Cooky.

But most of the time I wasn't involved in the conversations. When I was, and found myself pressed for thoughts or answers, I took out a mirror and combed my bangs. I found that I could just keep gazing and combing without having to meet anybody's eyes. Every now and then I'd insert a unh-unh or un-hunh, or ask "Do you like me better with bangs or without?" and that seemed to be enough of a contribution. Cooky and Gretel would just go on and talk. And talk and talk and talk.

Gretel to Cooky: "That Mary is really queer. She came right up to me at my locker and went *boing* with her boobs."

Cooky to Gretel: "Where? In front?"

Gretel shrugged.

Cooky (impatient for the facts): "In *front?*"

Gretel: "No, in back. But *boing, boing.*

Cooky (disinterested): "Yeah. She's odd. I always told you she was odd." (Taking powder, mascara, base, hair spray, and hairbrush from her satchel): "My mother's coming home tomorrow."

"I thought she wasn't coming home till Friday."

"No. Only one week. I told you. God, I've got to get the stains out of the coats."

"Why don't you tell her a big rat got in the closet?"

"Oh yeah, I can just see that. 'A big rat named Cooky,' she'd say. How do you get those stains out?"

And they went on. Talking and talking and talking.

Leaving class one day, both Cooky and Gretel warned me to watch out for colored girls. "They'll gang up on you," said Gretel. "They did that to me," said Cooky. "If they see you alone on the steps or in the halls, they'll close in on you. They got Sandy the other day, on the way home, right outside of school. The girls are worse than the boys. If they come up to you, keep moving."

She laughed at the expression on my face. "Didn't you have that in your school?" she asked.

I said we didn't.

"Well, watch out," she repeated.

The next afternoon, just as we took our seats in the auditorium, a Negro girl standing in the far right aisle asked Cooky what time it was. There was a clock on the wall about eight feet from where Cooky was sitting, and she looked up at it. Then she turned her back to the Negro girl and pretended to talk to Gretel.

"Hey," the girl said. "Did you hear me? I said what time is it?"

Without turning, Cooky coolly replied; "There's a clock right there."

The Negro girl walked to a spot in front of, and parallel to, Cooky's chair. She looked up at the clock and walked away. As she did so, Cooky and Gretel gave each other satisfied looks.

Two girls I hadn't seen before joined us that day. One plunked into a seat next to Gretel; the other sat on the arm of her chair. They were a pair of best friends. One was very pretty, with lots of brown hair and large green eyes. The other was plain and wore glasses. They had on similar skirts and blouses, and identical shoes. I learned, in due course, that they double-dated with their steadies, who were also best friends, they were taking the same courses, they shared all their thoughts, and they teased each other unmercifully, as though supporting each other with affectionate jabs. After every class they went some-

133

where to compare notes. If you happened to see one alone and ask where the other was, she'd know.

The pretty one spoke first. "I wanna go back to Catholic school," she said. "I can't stand this shitty dump."

"Gee, really?" said Cooky. "I would think Catholic school would be horrible. Don't they have a lot of rules and stuff?"

"Unh-unh," said Pretty Girl. "Well, they don't let you wear eye liner or rat your hair. But I don't rat mine anyway."

"It looks like you do," said Cooky.

"Well, I don't," she insisted. "I just tease it a little."

"I don't rat mine anymore, either," said Gretel.

"You big *liar*," said Cooky.

Gretel thumped her one. "Oh, you shut up, nut," she said.

"In New York they iron their hair," I volunteered.

Nobody believed me, but I insisted it was true. I told them you set the iron at Silk and iron your hair dry to make it straight and shiny. They gasped. (This custom has since earned national publicity; during my school days it was new and regional.)

Pleased that I had something to talk about, I attempted to go on with the subject. I had used up all my time, however. You only get about four inhales and three exhales per topic. Measured another way, you get approximately one and a half statements per topic. After that you can keep on talking, of course, but no one is listening. The conversational pace was roughly equal to the movement of a Ping-Pong ball bouncing across a cement floor. Thus:

"Hey, did you get a cat?"

"I don't like cats."

"I like dogs."

134

"Hey, I've got the same skirt you have. Turn around. Yeah. The same."

"Tony wasn't in English class today."

"He wasn't? Where was he?"

"Hey, did you see *The Rogues?* God, I wanted to see it and I missed it. Now it's off forever."

"Sue is still going with Nort."

"She *is?* God, I can't *stand* him."

"Did you see Finny? She cut her hair."

"Yeah. She's crazy."

"Are you going into town tomorrow?"

"Maybe. I have to see Sherry first and see if she wants to go because she said maybe her mother would take us and if she doesn't we might take the bus. Or if not, we might go to the library. Why?"

"I thought I might go."

"Oh."

"Hey, how much do you weigh?" (Here we get a slower bounce.)

"Why?" said Pretty Girl. "Do I look fat?"

"No," said Gretel, "I just wondered."

Pretty Girl: "One hundred twenty."

Gretel: "How tall are you?"

Pretty Girl: "Five four."

Gretel: "Eek. I'm five six and I only weigh a hundred and six."

Cooky: "Well, Gretel, you're *skinny.*"

Pretty Girl's friend was five feet two and weighed 106.

Cooky: "Oh, Gretel, you're not five six. Stand up."

Pretty Girl and Gretel stood up to measure themselves back to back, but first Pretty Girl had to take off her heels. Yop. Gretel was five six.

"Whadja give Alf for his birthday?"

"I'm getting him two sweaters. I didn't get them yet."

"What's he gonna give you? I know. Look out, Sandy.

135

Ha-ha. He's got a great present for you. Wait'll you see it."

"He already gave me that. Ha-ha."

"Which teacher did you get for gym?"

"I don't know yet. God, I hope it isn't Smiley. God, I'll *die* if I get her. She hates me. She wanted to throw me out last year but old Jenkins wouldn't let her."

"Are you going to the show Saturday?"

"I don't know. We went last week. Tommy *hated* it. Oh God, it was *so funny*. He got down on the floor of the car and wouldn't come up and we all pretended he wasn't there. Then Elk decided to drive out like that and all these people were staring at us because all they could see was these three heads and one arm hanging out the back."

"Oh that's *funny*. Whad they *do?*"

"Oh they kept staring and then we didn't look anymore but it was so funny. You would have died."

"Did you see Roxanne's purse?"

"No."

"Her aunt gave it to her. The one from Detroit."

"Let me have your base, will you?"

Silence.

Silence.

Silence.

There was panic in the air. Nobody knew what to say next. There was still plenty of time to make up, tease hair, discuss hair ribbons, examine insides of shoes, compare fingernails, condemn false eyelashes, look for chewing gum, long for a drag . . . and then there was *still* time.

"*Eeeeeeeh,*" shrieked the pretty girl. And again, "*Eeeeeeeh.*"

Gretel laughed. Everybody laughed.

"*Eeeeeeeh,*" shrieked the plain girl, kicking her foot against the side of the chair. "*Eeeeeeeh.* It's so boring in here."

"They're having one of their moods," explained Gretel. And finally, the bell rang and the girls scattered, promising all the way up the aisles that each would phone the other as soon as she got home.

The last Phys Ed talkathon took place in one of Urban's two gymnasiums, a huge, hollow room with the smell of thirty years of push-ups in its pores. More than a hundred girls were gathered there to be divided into four separate classes. The head gym teacher herded all into the center of the spar-varnished floor, and shouted for everyone to sit down and keep quiet. She would go over the rules of her classes just this once, and no one was ever to tell her "one merry day" that she couldn't be heard. While she talked, her aides patrolled the perimeter.

Her speech was belligerent, and maybe it had to be. Most teenage girls don't like gym. At least they claim they don't. The mere idea of gym class gives them the vapors. And they do go to a lot of trouble to get out of it. So the head gym teacher forewarned them:

"If you don't want to be here, *I don't want you.* If you don't want to be here, *speak up now* and I'll flunk you right now so you don't have to come back. If you decide to stay, you better know this: *You are to come to class prepared to participate.* You must have regulation gym suits, socks, and sneakers. You must use a locker for your clothes and *lock it.* You must take a shower before you leave, and I mean *every day of the month.* If you plan not to take a shower, ever, you must bring a written excuse from your doctor. Is that understood?"

Cooky and Gretel made faces at each other and giggled through their fingers. One of the aides walked over and gestured at them to behave. They waited until she turned her back and made faces again. Two other girls were giggling over a photograph. The aide sneaked up behind

137

them and they didn't see her. They didn't know she was there until she yanked the photograph out of their hands and put it in her pocket. She made one girl sit on one side of the room and the other stand against the wall.

The leader continued: "All equipment must be replaced in the allotted space. Lockers must be locked at all times because there are a lot of thieves around here. There are only two possible grades: FF or FU. Anybody who doesn't want to spend time in here can take her FU right now and go to the Dean's office." (That's what she said and I don't know what the initials stand for.)

When the proclamations were over, the narrow-limbed teachers strode from the room, leaving us to "talk quietly" until the bell rang. The division of classes would be posted on the wall by the end of the period, they said, and next time we came we'd better know what division we were in.

When they had gone, a hundred girls sat on the floor, glaring. There was complete silence for a moment; then a drone started low on the floor and rose, sounding like a million locusts, into the air.

"That bitch, why'd I have to get in *her* class?"

"My doctor'll give me an excuse. I'm not gonna go through *this* all year."

"That lousy les. Let her flunk me. Just let her."

"Christ, I hate that bitch."

That over, the girls began to move around to talk to their friends, take out their combs, check their mascara. Cooky and Gretel signaled me to join them, and we stood up to stretch our legs. The hundred girls sorted themselves out according to type and color; life went on. Pretty Girl and her best friend moseyed over to our corner, as did an innocent-looking blonde I had never seen before.

"Hey, do you like Scotch?" Pretty Girl asked Cooky. "I like gin and bourbon."

138

"I like gin-and-tonic," said Pretty Girl's friend.

"Oh, have you tried Bitter Lemon?" the frail blonde inquired. "It's really tough. *Oooooooh*. I *love* Bitter Lemon. With whiskey, it's *really* tough."

"Oh great. And with bourbon. Or Scotch-and-tonic," suggested Gretel.

Ping-Pong.

There was talk about Billy hating Fred, Roxanne pursuing Gretel's ex, Sharon sending pants to her steady in college and—from nowhere—talk of marriage and divorce.

Ping-Pong.

"If your parents don't get along, it's better if they get divorced," said Cooky.

"Do you miss your father?" Gretel asked me. "I used to miss mine, but he was kind of crude and loud. It's better if I don't see him."

"You have to look at it this way," Cooky said to me. "If your parents weren't getting divorced, you would never have gotten this trip. It's fun to travel."

Before we traveled out of gym class we checked the class lists on the bulletin board. Cooky and Gretel were together in Group B. I was in Group D with no one I knew, but several girls Gretel said were in Georgia's gang. Gretel was all sympathy. "Oh, poor you," she said.

"Wait'll you get a load of *them*," added Cooky.

Wait'll they get a load of me in my gym suit, I thought.

# 14

I wonder if we know how profoundly conditioned we become during our school years. I have observed vaguely in recent years that I act in some situations like a schoolgirl, or rather the way I did when I was a schoolgirl. I have found myself in relationships that were teacher-pupil, reacted to my bosses as though they were principals, applied homework methods to housework, and I have felt many times on many days that I was taking tests I could flunk or pass. But I had never had an inkling of the depth or extent of my responses to twelve years of public schooling. Furthermore, it is unlikely that I ever would have if I hadn't gone back to school—not as a visitor, but as a student. I could never have anticipated what would happen to my *mind* in this retreat. I could never have guessed that I would have moments of complete regression and that on some days I would feel about school that I had never left it at all. Perhaps I wouldn't have regressed if I had found going to school very different from what I once knew it to be. But, as I've pointed out rather frequently in these pages, I did not find that the brave new world had arrived at Urban High. The old familiar one was still there in a surprising number of corners. And every time I collided with it I reacted, as any child might observe, like some kind of nut.

The first two days of school I was so nervous about getting caught I was rigid. By the third day, though, I was running to classes and not because I was afraid I'd be discovered, but because I was afraid to be tardy. I didn't walk into a class, I skidded in as if I were stealing a base.

By the fourth day I was afraid of some of my teachers, heaven help me, and by the end of the first week I was trying to figure out ways to get around doing my homework. That's about the time, too, I developed a genuine slouch and an adolescent skin condition. Glory hallelujah, why was my *skin* regressing? Because I was sneaking candy bars all day for energy, and because I was wearing so bloody much makeup.

You can't imagine the number of chemical compounds I was putting on my face between 7 A.M. and midnight. Pancake makeup covered with liquid makeup covered with cream makeup, under which there was white goo that's supposed to disguise rings under the eyes, over which there was brush-on rouge and brush-on base and puffed-on pressed powder. Over which there was all that hair I was trying to hide under.

You've heard about boys getting acne these days from the bangs they're wearing? Well, so do girls, if you will permit me the euphemism.

My skin might have survived the onslaught, I suppose, if I had given it a few hours of rest once in a while. But I never gave up hoping to find something that would restore the wash-and-wear face I had many years ago. Nearly every day I bore home some new miracle formula from the drugstore on the corner where I changed buses. Creams to melt the years away, lotions to dry them away, pastes to tighten them away, acids to flake them off. I was

141

particularly fond of the one that was supposed to give a six-hour face lift. It went on wet and would purportedly lift your laugh lines (?) as it dried. An old Indian torture, I think. Old Indians used to tie wet leather bands around the foreheads of captives and then put them out in the sun to dry. That was the first head-shrinking known to man, I'm told. (Bess told me.) Well, I put this facial on one day after school and I couldn't talk or smile until the end of the late, late show. I think it was embalming fluid; it didn't erase my wrinkles, it preserved them for posterity.

The most shocking signs of my regression, however, were not on my face but in my behavior, particularly in Spanish class, where on two outstanding occasions I found myself totally out of control. The first incident might have had something to do with adult responses; the second could not possibly have.

The first occurred when I was forced to participate openly in a class activity. On a prescheduled day, each person in the room had to do an individual recitation of a short poem we had been learning to recite together in Spanish. It was my first solo of any nature at Urban. Each of us had to get up, go to the front of the room, face the class, and recite. Our order was alphabetical, as usual, and so I went through most of the period just listening. As I did so I was quite relaxed, almost indifferent. I knew the poem well; I'd memorized it before I went to sleep the night before, and gone over it again in the morning in study hall. But when Miss Zorri nodded, indicating it was my turn, I began to shake so badly I could barely get out of the chair. I broke out in a sweat and I'm sure I changed color.

I turned to face the class and stared straight at my toes. I didn't know what to do with my hands. I didn't know where to look. I couldn't get any volume into my voice. When I started on the first line, Miss Zorri asked me to

142

speak louder, so I backed up with a cough and began again, this time fixing my sights on the yellow overhead light nearest the window.

I got to the end of the first phrase and . . . blank. I couldn't remember the next word; not even the next initial. The boys in rows three and four laughed. I got redder.

Miss Zorri prompted me and I went another two phrases. Then blank again. So the boys laughed louder and Miss Zorri threw me another cue. I finally stumbled to the end of the poem and sat down, too embarrassed to show any sign of life.

What was the poem?

*Treinta dias tiene septiembre*
*Abril, junio, y noviembre.*
*Los que sobran tienen treinta y uno*
*Excepto febrero que tiene veinte y ocho.*

"Thirty days has September, April, June, and November. . . ."

The girl in front of me recited it perfectly and she was only a sophomore.

"Take out paper and pencil" was the opening line of the second incident. That line. To hear it again intoned in the same icy, indisputable way I had heard it all through my youth was a Technicolor nightmare. We were about to have a flash quiz on two verbs I hadn't studied. The gull feathers I felt in the pit of my stomach as I looked at the blank piece of paper on my desktop were at least seventeen years old. So was my initial action. Without a moment of rational thought, I tried to see the paper on the desk of the girl on my left and copy what was on it. Furthermore, I succeeded.

143

I cheated. Me, the married woman with a home and responsibilities and a Social Security number and an alligator bag. I cheated. And not because I was afraid to bring undue attention to Lyn Tornabene, spy journalist, but because I was afraid to be a bad student. It hadn't been a year since the last time I tsk-tsk'd over newspaper reports of mass cheating in schools in various parts of the country, and there I was, being a startling statistic.

Had I cheated so spontaneously when I was a real student? I must assume, now, that I had. Otherwise I'd have to believe that I felt more pressure to succeed the second time I went to high school than the first. And that's unthinkable.

Isn't it?

Remembering—really remembering—leaves so little to tsk-tsk about.

The other weird thing, and I mean *weird*, was the gradual but distinct change in Bess's attitude toward me. Little by little she began to treat me like a child. I noticed this first in her voice, then in her actions, and finally in her panicky efforts to protect and discipline me.

In the beginning I thought she was kidding. She is a kind of larky, Auntie Mame character, and our relationship has always been a mutually respectful, rather drawing-room-comedy one. I was always particularly fond of her sense of the ridiculous, her vigor in ferreting out life's fine madnesses.

And so of course the first week of Operation Teenager brought out the comedian in her. She broke up just looking at me. Then, I suppose, she got used to the sight of me in my school clothes or blue jeans, hanging around the house with a textbook in my hand.

We could never go out to a movie together or to a restaurant because we might run into someone she knew or, worse yet, someone I knew—like, for instance, Gretel. She did confide in one close friend besides David's mother, and we did go to the nice lady's house for dinner one night. That was the evening I decided my derangement was catching.

Let me assure you that clothes do the woman make, that you are what you wear, and that even if they can't, people do judge a book by its cover. Bess and her friend at first made jokes about my belted trench coat, adorable skirt, neatly starched shirt, and Prince Valiant haircut. But then they began to look at me very strangely. By the end of dinner they were asking odd questions about how was school today and pausing, not knowing what else to say, the way adults tend to talk to sixteen-year-olds. I tried to bring them around to reality by pouring myself a bourbon-on-the-rocks and mentioning my husband and the time we ran into this couple we knew from home right in the middle of the Ponte Vecchio—but no go. I found them stopping each other from talking about their dates, and trying not to curse, and sneaking off to the kitchen for serious discussions away from the children.

Oh yes, I forgot to mention. Bess's friend had a precocious seven-year-old son who wasn't helping matters any. I loved him on sight and he me. "Little girl . . ." he would say, calling me to his room to paint with him. "Can that little girl come in after supper and play with me?" he asked his mommy. She answered, "No, dear, Lyn has to go home early tonight because she has school tomorrow. Maybe she can come over the weekend to play with you." And by God, right after dinner Bess carted me home to see that I did my homework and got my rest.

The tone Bess used when she suggested I shape up for David's visit was also quite typical. "Straighten up . . . take off your glasses . . ." Who says that to an adult? Except somebody's mother. And that's what Bess was

145

turning into. A complementary metamorphosis, that's what it was. Her concern about my not having any dates grew less and less larky as time went on. "You're not bad-looking," she observed, "but you have a personality disorder." And she laughed, but she also worried.

After my social life got rolling, both with my gang and with David, Bess showed a new brand of anxiety. She seemed to fear that I was going to get into some kind of trouble—become an unwed mother or start smoking pot; I'm not sure precisely what. She really did seem to feel that she was responsible for a child who was far from home and prey to all kinds of wickedness. It didn't matter how often I reminded her that I was thirty-four and insured.

One night she brought home a tale about the fifteen-year-old daughter of a friend of hers who was quite wealthy and socially prominent. This child, she told me with horror, had picked up a young soldier at the movies and was having a serious romance with him. The child's mother didn't know what to do to break them up and she was getting ill over it. Bess was upset about it, too, to the point of not being able to talk about anything else for several consecutive evenings.

"Do you think this has something to do with me?" I finally asked her.

She shrugged.

"Now, come on," I said. "Do you think I might pick up a soldier, too? Me? Your old buddy from the big city?"

She shrugged again. "How do I know what might happen to you when you're out with those kids?" she said. "If you were late I wouldn't even know who to call. We don't even have Gretel's phone number."

"I can't ask for her number unless I offer her mine," I said.

Bess said she realized that. "Maybe we can find it

anyway," she suggested. "You know her last name and the neighborhood where she lives; let's see what we can do with the phone book."

There were two families bearing Gretel's last name. I called the first and the man who answered said he was Gretel's uncle. He told me I could reach her at the other number, and for the moment, that was all I wanted to know. Both Bess and I made note of it. This made her feel better, but not for long.

It was inevitable that there would be sporadic bursts of teenage trouble once school was under way. And there were. Inevitably, they made the front pages of the local papers. Inevitably, they made Bess frantic.

HIGH SCHOOL STUDENT STOLE OUT OF FEAR. That was the headline on the first story. It stretched across the front page of the evening paper Bess brought home and tossed dramatically in my direction. The student in question was a boy, a junior at Urban High. He had been caught stealing money from the cash register in his uncle's hardware store. At the police station he confessed he had been stealing regularly to pay off a gang of senior boys who threatened to beat him up either if he stopped paying them or if he told anyone about them.

Bess responded to the headline with fury about today's teenagers in general and the ones attending my high school in particular. I did something I didn't expect to do. I got angry. My objectivity went in a rush of school spirit I didn't know I had. I lost, as they say on the mall, my cool, and began insisting to a contemporary with whom I was normally intellectually compatible that my school was a good school and my kids were good kids.

"I guess you know what you're doing," Bess said. "But personally, I think you should drop out of that place before something odd happens to you."

On that note she went to dress for a dinner date and a

147

half hour later dashed out with a smile and a flip "Don't stay up too late. If you're a good girl I'll drive you to school in the morning, but you'll have to get up early and have breakfast with me."

I felt strange and lonely after she'd gone. I wanted company, someone with whom I could talk out my feelings about these kids I was defending. Strangest of all, it was their company I really wanted. Though I didn't know what to say to them, at least when I was with them I had a status.

Comfort was at hand. I had Gretel's phone number. I could call her. That's what the kids did when they were alone in an adult environment—they just picked up the phone, that little yellow blanket, and held on to it until they felt secure again. "The next thing you know, lady," I said to myself, "you'll be sucking your thumb." But I put the phone in my lap anyway.

I dialed and a voice, played on black keys only, said hello.

"Hi, Gretel, it's me. Lyn," I said in falsetto.

"*Lyn?*" she screeched. "Hey. *Hi.* Where did you get my phone number?"

"My guardian found it for me," I chirped.

"She *did?* Gee. Well, how'd she find it?"

I could see we were off to a bad start. It was a mistake for me to have done anything so enterprising as to spend time searching for her. A real teenager would exert such effort only if the object of the search were a boy.

"Well, you told me where you lived and, well, she just found it. I don't know." I tried to giggle.

"Gee," she said. And then she was silent.

"Hey, did you see the paper tonight?" I asked quickly.

"Unh-unh, but my mother told me about it. Awful, isn't it?"

"Gee, terrible," I said. "Do you know that boy?"

"Unh-unh, do you? Listen," she said, "do you want to go shopping with me after school Thursday? You can get your gym suit and maybe some shoes. Anyway we could look at shoes."

"Gee, I'd love to."

"Would you?"

"Gee, yes. I really would."

"That's swell, then. Wear something dressy, not *too* dressy, but nice. You know. We always get dressed to go downtown. But listen, don't you have to ask your guardian? Maybe she won't let you."

"Oh, gee, I forgot. I do. But I think she'll let me."

"Do you think so?"

"Gee, I *think* so."

"What time do you have to get home?"

"What time do *you* have to get home?"

"Five. We eat early."

"We do, too," I said.

"Okay, swell, then. We both have to be home at five."

(That won't give us much time, I thought; but I didn't say so.)

"Listen," I said. "Are you going to the football game at Seth?"

"Unh-unh," she said. The reason, she explained, was that her family always got together for dinner Friday—"all my aunts and uncles and everything"—and she had to get home right after school.

I didn't believe her. The football game was at three and she could have been home in time for dinner if she had to be. More than likely her mother wouldn't let her go because it was out of town, but she would never say that because that would give her mother a bad image. Gretel used her mother only when she needed a quotable authority to avoid doing something she didn't want to do anyway.

149

I moaned with disappointment and sympathy, and she giggled. "Well you know how it *is*."

I giggled. "Yes, I do."

She giggled Then there was silence.

"Well, listen, I've got to go now," I said.

"Is your guardian in the room?"

"Ummm."

Gretel giggled again. "I got it," she said. "I've got to go, too."

"Your mother there?"

"Uh-huh." Giggle.

"Okay. Bye, then."

"Bye," she said. "See you in English tomorrow."

"Oh, that's right," I said.

"You crazy, you forgot."

"Gee, I did."

"Bye, then," she said.

"Bye," I repeated.

I put the receiver on its hook and went cheerfully to the refrigerator to begin making dinner. For some odd reason, I felt like myself again. I was hungry. And I was curious. I wanted to turn on the radio and hear news about the big wide world. Just as I reached for the radio, though, I had a queer flash. What if when I flip this button, I thought, I find out there's an all-out war between those umpty million teenagers out there and the rest of us? Whose side will I be on?

I believe I can say with accuracy that when I was sixteen years old I spent 80 per cent of the hours I was awake, and at home, on the telephone. Just for instance, every single Sunday of my junior year I lay on the dining room floor at the feet of the telephone table, my own feet on the ledge of a highboy, for a minimum of three hours, during which I was in constant communication with the seven other members of my gang. The object of the calls was to plan the day. I would pick up the phone and hear:

"Hi. Marilyn? Hi. It's Joanna."

"Oh, hi, Jo-Jo. How was the movie?"

"Oh great. Listen, I'll tell you about it later. What're we doing today?"

"I don't know. What shall we do? Did you speak to Nancy?"

"No, not yet. I wanted to call you first. Do you have the car?"

"I don't know. I didn't ask yet. I was going to find out if Carolyn had the car. Can you get your car?"

"I don't know. It depends on what we're doing."

"Well, listen. Why don't you call Nancy and see what she's doing? Then I'll call Carolyn and see if she has the car and call you back. Okay?"

"Okay. I'll call Nancy right now."

"Okay. And I'll call Carolyn. Bye."

"Bye."

"Hi. Carolyn? It's Marilyn."

"No kidding? I thought it was Tyrone Power. Listen, shithead, I just called you and your line was busy."

"Yeah, I know. I was talking to Jo-Jo."

"Oh great. Did she like the movie?"

"I think so. She said it was great, but you know Jo-Jo. Listen, do you have the car today?"

"I don't know. What're we doing?"

"I don't know yet."

"Did you talk to Jo?"

"No, not yet."

"Well, maybe she has the car and then I won't have to ask for mine. I don't know if I can have it because Alice has to go to choir later."

"Well, Jo-Jo said maybe she could get the car if you

151

couldn't. But I think maybe I can get ours and we can pick Jo up later."

"Well, it would be easier if Jo had the car, wouldn't it? Because then she could drop us all off and go straight home instead of you or Jo-Jo having to take her home and then go back."

"Yes. That's right. But where should we go?"

"I don't know. Why don't you call Jo and then call me back? I'll call Sue if you want me to, and see if she wants to come here. Then we can wait for you at my house."

"Okay. You call Sue and I'll call Jo and then you call me back."

"Okay. Bye."

"Bye."

"Hi. Marilyn? It's Cathy . . ."

"Hi, Gretel, it's Lyn . . ."

Only the names had changed.

The morning after the night before, the lead story in the paper was about a junior in a high school on the other side of the city. Again there was a banner headline, this time announcing TEENAGER STABBED IN SCHOOL. The report in the upper-right corner said it was a racial fight: several members of a Negro gang had set upon a white boy in a rival gang. It was a disturbing story. There was considerable racial tension in schools throughout the city, the paper claimed, and a bad year was anticipated. "Undoubtedly the first of many incidents to come," the paper termed the stabbing.

Bess was shaken. She asked me not to go to school for at least a day or two. "Wait till things calm down," she pleaded. Then she drove me to school without another word.

You know how sometimes you hear or read something shattering and go outside expecting the world to look different? That was my expectation as I walked through the gates and waited by a pillar for the bell to ring. I was sure everybody would be talking in hushed tones about the stabbing or the stealing. I expected something to show even in the posture of the early arrivers who always hung around making the courtyard look like the lunch-break scene from *Carmen*.

But everything was the same. The waiting games, the mating games, were proceeding as usual. So it went all day. In Spanish class I asked the girl in front of me if she knew the boy who was stabbed. She shrugged and shook her head no. At lunch I waited for mention of the stories, some indication that even if the kids weren't disturbed their parents were. Nothing. In gym class, the daily talkathon, no sign, no word.

In speech class there was a disturbance I was sure would prompt some scare talk. Right after the period got under way, Mr. Roth stopped in the middle of a sentence and stared at the door. Then he jumped up, opened the door, and yelled, "Hey, just a minute. What are you doing out here?"

We all looked toward the door and saw, in the shadows beyond Mr. Roth, a tall husky boy with long hair and a zippered jacket.

"What's your name?" Mr. Roth barked.

We couldn't hear the answer.

"You're not from this school. Are you?" Mr. Roth demanded. There was a pause. "Then what are you doing here?"

He flung the door open fully and ordered the boy to stand there without moving. Then he backed into the room, keeping his eyes on the boy, and picking up a wall phone, asked for the principal's office. When he got a reply, he said, "This is Bill Roth. I'm on my way down

153

with a young man who's been wandering around the halls. I don't know who he is or what he's doing here. I'll be downstairs in about two minutes."

He turned to the class. "I'll be back in a moment," he said. "Just read your textbooks. Abe, I'll make you responsible here. See that there's no noise." Then he took the stranger by the arm and led him away. He barely reached the boy's shoulder.

Abe had no problem with the class. As soon as Mr. Roth shut the door, the entire group did as it was told: read. Some read textbooks; others read *Lord of the Flies*. When Mr. Roth returned, class resumed as though nothing at all had happened. He lectured and we took notes. We learned that Hitler had a sense of humor, that Joe Kennedy bought John Kennedy the Presidency, that Churchill had a lisp, and that the United Fruit Company has plantations all through the Caribbean where they pay the natives eleven cents a day for picking bananas. We did not learn what had occurred when Mr. Roth went to the principal's office.

# 15

Kids' allowances and other forms of income are now smashing all records. The Gilbert firm reports that last year youngsters raked in a grand total of $13 billion, nearly double the figure of a decade before. By 1970, the total is expected to hit $20 billion.
—This Week Magazine, September 27, 1964

With a collective $15 billion a year to spend, the nation's 24 million teenagers have become the long-haired darlings of businessmen looking for big markets now and more when the young people begin setting up homes of their own.

"Teenagers have replaced farmers as the economic backbone of the nation," Mrs. Helen Nelson, California's consumer counsel reports. . . .

As Bruce A. Gimbel, department store president, put it: "We no longer keep up with the Joneses, we keep up with the young."
—Associated Press feature by Sally Ryan, February 9, 1966

155

The first shopping trip I had scheduled with Gretel loomed in my mind as one of the most important events of my second school days, and I planned to note every minute of it. To go, as a number-one song on the mid-nineteen-sixties song charts directed, "downtown, da da da *da* da-*da*" and participate in the rite that was allegedly maintaining America's economy, seemed a most awesome privilege indeed. I dressed for the occasion, as instructed by Gretel, in my best jumper. She wore the plaid suit that was just like Mrs. Cramer's. We met at her locker, picked up Billy, Roxanne, and Kelly in the john, and then joined the crowd leaving the school grounds for the day.

My classmates were quite a sight at 3:15 P.M. They erupted from school in groups of friends and steadies and streamed down all the streets that led to the bus stops like lava down a mountain. There was no morning hesitation in their stride. They had the force of springs uncoiling. They were not docile like the people who leak out of glass-walled office buildings at five-thirty. They were noisy, physical—almost wild. You could no more turn them back than you could halt a tidal wave.

The adults on the streets around Urban didn't like the sight of the kids leaving school. They backed off in fear and hostility to let them pass. I saw the hostility on the street. I felt it after school in the company of my young friends.

When I got on a bus with them I could feel the current: Ugh—teenagers. Look out—teenagers. I could understand why they clung together and laughed out loud and carried on to show how unaffected they were by all the hostility in the air. I understood it even better at the close of the shopping trip.

Billy, Roxanne and Kelly were going with us only as far as the bus stop; they all had to be home early. On the way to the stop, Gretel pointed out an area where, she said, the

156

tough Negro girls hung around after school. "We have to pass there," she said. "When we do, just keep moving and don't look around. Watch out, especially, for the drug-store and the candy store. There are always a whole bunch of them in the doorways."

I felt some vague fear as we started up the block, primarily because I didn't know what to expect. My friends didn't change their pitch but they accelerated their pace, as though they were passing a haunted house. I fell behind them. Suddenly a Negro girl stepped out of the entrance to a store and blocked my path.

"You're the new kid, aren't you?" she said.

I nodded.

Gretel stopped up ahead of me and gestured for me to move, but I couldn't without deliberately stepping around the girl. She didn't look as if she meant me any harm. She was waiting for a reaction. I stepped to the side and she put her hand on my arm to stop me.

"Gimme a Kent," she said.

I looked to Gretel for a sign. She nodded, so I reached into my pocketbook for a cigarette and handed it to the girl. She took it without looking at it and then, as unex-pectedly as she had appeared, she stepped back to let me pass. I smiled with relief and walked on. She called after me, "Hey, baby, you old enough to smoke? Does your mother know you smoke?"

I turned back and smiled, shaking my head no.

Gretel pulled me forward. "I told you not to stop," she said with angry concern. "Don't answer her. There's a whole bunch of them in that store and they'll be out here any minute. You looking for trouble? Come on." She galloped ahead, forcing me to run to catch up.

At the bus stop, where the rest of the gang watched anxiously for us, we came to a halt. Billy grabbed Gretel in a kind of hug, and Roxanne and Kelly closed around

157

me. They giggled and shouted, making a boisterous show of camaraderie. Then they broke into frenetic dance steps and confused me completely. I had thought the show was being put on for the benefit of the Negro girls a half block behind us, but this was the action I had come to recognize as part of the mating rites. Were there boys around? Yes. Downwind. Elaborately paying no attention to the girls whatsoever.

One of them, I found out via a large poke in the ribs from Kelly, was Gretel's ex. My not recognizing him was a very big social gaffe.

There was an interesting backdrop for this scene. Directly behind Billy was a newspaper rack. In it was a weatherworn paper with its banner headline still shouting TEENAGER STABBED IN SCHOOL.

"Gee, look," I said, pointing to the paper.

The girls glanced at it. "Yeah," said Gretel. "Terrible, isn't it?" Then she went on dancing, shouting goodbye as she did so to Billy, Roxanne and Kelly, who ran to get on their bus and disappeared.

The next incident happened so quickly I still can't quite figure it out.

A bus stopped in front of us—that I know. Gretel said, "C'mon, this is ours," and I looked down into my pocketbook for my ticket. When I looked up Gretel was gone and the bus door was shut. All in a flash. I pounded on the door and shouted. As I did so, the bus pulled away. I ran after it for half a block, shouting at it in total disbelief. Gretel waved to me out the window, cheering me on to the next bus stop nearly two blocks away. I didn't even try to make it. I stopped dead in the middle of the street and stood there feeling like an idiot. Stupidly, I had never thought to ask Gretel where, precisely, we were going. I couldn't hop on another bus and meet her downtown because I didn't know where that was, and, mysteriously, there was not a soul around to ask. It was farce, pure and simple, and it got worse.

There, running toward me up the street, was Gretel. She had pulled the emergency strap and leaped from the bus like Superfriend. She was in a terrible state, having been torn, as it turned out, between her impulse to rescue me and her passionate need to stay on the bus. For on the bus was—can you imagine *who?* Her *ex.* I had made her miss the bus on which her *ex* was riding. A person should die for such a thing. *"Oooooooh. Eeeeeee. Awwwwwww."* (I think those were her words.)

*"He was right there and I could have ridden downtown with him and maybe he would have stayed with us and* OOOOOOOH! How did it happen? What happened? Where were you? Oh, that terrible bus driver. Oh. Oh. And he heard you pounding on the door and I screamed at him to let you on and he just drove away. Like that. It was so terrible, so horrible. I could *kill* him. If I ever see him again I'll *kill* him. Oh, if I'd just gotten his name. Oh oh oh. It'll never happen again like that, just never. Oh oh oh."

Was ever a heart so broken? I didn't know what to do for her. I didn't know what to say. I could only listen, all the way downtown, to her lament. So many blows in a day. So much to bear. "I know," I told her. "I know."

Despite our grief, we made it to town.

Gretel's mother had given her an extra dollar to spend on our spree and she planned to invest it in a pair of "crazy stockings." Her regular allowance was six dollars a week, which had to cover the thirty-five cents or so she spent every day for lunch. It was the same amount most of the kids got, she said, but it wasn't "very much." She spent most of it, as far as she could figure, on makeup, movies, and records.

She had charge accounts in all the stores. "All the kids have them," she said. "You'll have to get some, too." Her mother went with her on all major shopping trips, a fact she resented, but only mildly. "My mother always wants me to buy clothes too big so I can grow into them. But I'm not going to grow that way anymore. You know, we get taller and thinner and nothing fits right. We're changing shape. She doesn't understand that."

Our main project was to get me a gym suit, so we did that first, skipping up the escalator of the main department store to the fourth-floor sportswear department.

"May I help you?" inquired a sweet-faced, gray-haired little lady.

I flinched. It was a twice-conditioned reflex. I drew away from the nice lady both because I was afraid she'd look at me and gasp "Why, you're no child," and because, like all New York shoppers, I have learned to be defensive with salesladies.

"What size gym suit would you like?" the lady asked. I said I wasn't sure. She picked up a handful in a variety of sizes and suggested, tenderly, that I try them all on to make sure I chose one that was roomy and comfortable.

I wondered what her game was and stayed on the defensive.

Did I want a nice, cozy, warm sweatshirt, too, for the chilly days I'd be playing outside? "We have two regulation styles." I said no, thank you, to the sweat shirt, waiting for the lady to slam my hand in the drawer, as was Their habit. But she didn't reject me at all. She stayed sweet and loving and concerned, insisting I go into a nice dressing room and take my time and buy the right gym suit.

Well, I didn't want to go to the dressing room because I knew that Gretel would have to come along to cast her vote. It would have been unforgivable of me to leave her alone.

160

"I think she'll wear the nine," Gretel said to the sales-lady. "She's so *tiny*." Then she bundled me off to the dressing room.

I undressed without taking any clothes off, which is a trick I learned at age eleven in a badly heated YWCA. It didn't really matter because Gretel wasn't watching me anyway. There was a full-length mirror in the dressing room; she was watching it.

"Do you like my hair better with or without the band?" she inquired as I scrambled into the size 9 (too small, try the 11).

I studied her head. "Without," I said.

"Ummmm," she stumbled. She took off her glasses and stepped closer to the mirror, put the glasses on and stepped back from the mirror. Then she put on the head band.

I bought the size 11 for $4.14 including tax, and graciously accepted the saleslady's profuse thanks. I still own that horror with the bloomers. Someday I'll wear it on the tennis court and win by default.

The gym suit matter thus settled, Gretel then made sure I became acquainted with every vital department of every store in town. Her favorite spots were the cosmetics counters, where she lingered long and hungrily. She checked every new lipstick color and striped the most interesting ones down the back of her hand. She sniffed powders and bases, trying all those in sample containers. "Sometimes a couple of us spend all day Saturday at makeup demonstrations," she said, spraying herself with one bottle after another of cologne. "One of us gets all this crazy stuff put on for free, and we just have a ball." The gang also liked to get all dressed up and try on clothes in the designer departments. They *loved* department stores, she said. She would like to live in one.

Gretel was becoming very frustrated in her search for new stockings. The only pair she cared for so far was already owned by Cooky, and that ruled them out. "Cooky would *kill* me if I bought these," she said. "But they're *darling*, aren't they? Why don't you buy them?"

I told her I didn't have enough money and she accepted that. I don't know why I could buy the stockings that she couldn't buy.

There were two shoe stores in town that couldn't have done better if they were barreling their own oil. One was out of bounds for the likes of me and Gretel. I was allowed to look in its window, but not pass through its portals. Shoes there were around five dollars a pair. In the nice girls' shoe store, where we shopped, shoes averaged around eight dollars a pair and were very much like the five-dollar ones, only more refined. I was very amused at myself looking in those windows. I had thought the girls at school were wearing a remarkable variety of shoe styles and planned to say so. "No conformity here," I had thought smugly. But every pair of shoes I had seen at Urban had come from one of these two shoe stores. The brand name of the shoe didn't count (Gretel had never heard of Pappagallos), nor did the style. It was the store that mattered.

We stared in the windows of the store of our caste, trying to find a pair of heels that looked like me. "Sherry has those," said Gretel about a pair I liked. I pointed to another pair. "Billy has those." Point again: Ann has those." Point, point: "Kelly has those in brown, Georgia in red, Liza in black. *Everybody* has the other pair." Point: "Oh, those are neee-*ew!* Oh, they're kee-*ute!* Oh, they must have just come in. Oh, get the number. You've got to get *those.*"

A salesman met us at the door and escorted us to a plush seat. The wall-to-wall-carpeted store was filled with teenagers. The salesman bowed and smiled and did a buck-and-wing. This was too much. The last time a shoe salesman had talked to me in New York, it was to tell me they don't make the kind of shoes I wear anymore.

Gretel told the man what shoes I wanted. He ran to get them and ran back, bubbling with happiness.

"These are just right for a little girl like you," he said, gently helping me off with my loafers.

"She's not a little girl," snapped Gretel.

"I mean, I mean small, er, short, er, tiny feet. Pretty. Pretty feet. Small. See?"

Gretel forgave him.

I bought the shoes and made Gretel's day. "Oh, I'm so happy for you," she said. "I know just what you'll go through tomorrow when everybody sees them. Everybody'll say 'Oh, they're *cute*.' Just you wait. You'll have such fun."

I am obligated to elaborate here. You see, "everybody" knew I was going shoe-hunting because I had said so at lunch. When Gretel got home she would telephone the report on our trip, thereby alerting all eyes to my feet. When I would arrive in school in the morning, if the new shoes were found on me, appropriate comments would be made. Thus did it happen the next morning—and all day long—that everybody did indeed examine my shoes and say "Oh, they're cute." They also said, "Oh, let's *see* them. Oh, how tough." One girl told me that she loved my shoes without looking at them. She knew just from hearing about them that she loved them.

In the last store we perused before we had to go home, Gretel found a pair of ribbed stockings for $1.50, which she said she *loved*. She carefully thought over what she might wear them with, decided they were practical as well as "tough," and made her one purchase for the day.

While we stood still for a moment waiting for her change, it dawned on me that I was completely exhausted. Playing the game, shopping in such a frenzy, paying attention—the combination had done me in. I could barely move. Gretel walked me to my bus stop, chattering every single step of the way, and I couldn't even summon the strength to nod my head. She had to be home from dates with strangers at eleven, she said. If she went out with her boyfriend, though, she could stay out till twelve. How about me?

"Yes."

She told me her ex was terribly moody, and not really in very good health. She had given him the best years of her life, she said. And she went on and on. Most of these intimate facts she prefaced with "Don't tell anybody, but . . ." which means, among the Young Ones, that what's being said isn't necessarily true.

Finally she left me on the right corner for my bus, told me to call her later, and went home. It was rush hour. Stores were closing, offices were disgorging workers, ladies who had been shopping queued up for buses. I longed to hail a cab but I didn't know if there were any in this city. Teenagers don't hail cabs. They don't even think about such things. Hailing a cab is a privilege of age.

The line on the corner was growing, and I shifted my books from hip to hip in an effort to keep from falling asleep on my feet. I hoped I'd have time to take a nap before I had to do my homework. Out of the corner of my left eye, I caught sight of myself in a shopwindow. There I stood, among a crowd of beautifully groomed women in real clothes, my dress hanging unevenly from beneath my belted trench coat, my hair hanging unevenly over my face, my face looking peculiarly misplaced on my body. I turned away and then turned back again out of perverse curiosity, the way you look without really wanting to at an accident. The contrast between me and the other women was shocking. I really was a bug.

In the crowded bus I stood up rather than race an old

lady of at least thirty for a seat. And I confess, I stood there thinking about how I longed to go all the way home, back to my husband, back to my kitchen, back to my blue velvet couch, back to the life which had more shape and form and dimension than I had ever known it had. I could not, of course, go home yet. But the fact that I had work to do couldn't stop me from being glad I was not young anymore. On the bus heading away from downtown, that's how I felt.

# 16

SCHOOL ENDED a half hour early for students holding tickets to the football game with Urban's old rival, Seth High, the only high school in a small town some twenty miles away. The game began at four in Seth's stadium. Three chartered buses waited to transport Urbanites there. None, however, would be waiting to take them away.

"How are we going to get home from the game?" I had asked my friends.

Kelly was the only one who answered. "Oh, somehow or other," she had said. "Don't worry, we'll find a way when we get there. But bring a dollar in case we get stranded."

The plan was for Kelly, Roxanne, Billy and me to meet at Urban's north gate where the buses were loading. Billy and Roxanne were waiting when I got there. I had never seen Roxanne without Kelly before. She looked like one of a pair of salt and pepper shakers. She had on her usual moon clothes but they looked more bizarre than usual next to Billy's conservative blazer, skirt and sweater. I wore a button-down shirt, plaid skirt, fuzzy sweater and huge sunglasses like Kelly's, which my friends said looked neat. Kelly, it was assumed, was being detained in gym class. "That bitch never lets anybody out early," said Billy, referring to the gym teacher. "Goddam her. She's such a *bitch.*"

Roxanne was upset by the absence of her chum. She paced back and forth, straining to see if she could catch a glimpse of her in the courtyard. Billy thought we should get on the bus, but Roxanne wouldn't. She didn't want to go if Kelly wasn't going, and she was afraid Kelly would be too late even for the last bus. When the lead bus started warming up, Billy insisted that we leave. Roxanne hung behind, then scampered to catch up with us, looking back anxiously all the way.

As we pulled away from Urban, the mood inside the bus was so high the vehicle could have soared aloft like a balloon without ballast. There were joyous shrieks of "Let's go" and "Hooray," and then just plain joyous shrieks. Every face except the bus driver's was lighted by an ear-to-ear grin. Even I felt the kinetic anticipation in the air. The kids were high on it. They were on their own, on the road; anything could happen. Until we were well beyond the city limits they did nothing but lurch in the aisles, giggling like happy drunks. Then, when the bus reached the open highway, the bus driver got adamant about his passengers settling down, so they did, relatively speaking. Billy, Roxanne and I stood among the band members. They didn't know anyone on the bus more than casually. I pointed out one of the cheerleaders who was in my home room; Billy said he was "a total ass." Then she complained of "*dreadful* fatigue," and looked around for a place to sit. She asked a boy with a tuba if he'd mind moving his damn horn and sat sideways with her feet in the aisle between me and Roxanne.

"How do you like it here now?" she asked me.

I shrugged and told her I was getting used to it.

"I bet you hated to leave New York," Roxanne said. I shrugged again. "I was in New York once," she said.

"So was I," said Billy.

"How'd you like it?" I asked.

"Oh, it was neat," said Roxanne.

"Really neat," echoed Billy.

"What did you like best?" I asked.

They thought a moment. "Well, I only saw Long Island," said Billy. "We flew in and went right to my aunt's house and it was night so I didn't see much."

"I was only five," said Roxanne. "But I'm going to go back someday."

"So am I," said Billy. "I'll bet you miss your friends."

I nodded.

"Did you go steady?" asked Roxanne.

"Sort of," I said.

"What was his name?"

"Frank."

"How old is he?"

"Oh, older. Nineteen."

Roxanne looked both impressed and sympathetic. "Gee," she said. "Do you write to him?"

I nodded.

"Gee, I'll bet you hated to leave him."

A boy behind a set of drums lit a cigarette and Billy immediately wanted one. She didn't have any, and neither did Roxanne. I did, but I wasn't sure if I should say so. Then Roxanne looked me straight in the eye and asked me if I had any cigarettes. I nodded.

"Are we allowed to smoke?" I asked.

Billy made a face at me. "Oh come on," she said. "What could happen? There's nobody on this bus. The bus driver can't even see us."

I palmed a cigarette, lit it, took a dramatic drag, and

168

passed it to Billy. She took a dramatic drag and handed it to Roxanne, who likewise took a dramatic drag. A boy standing near her poked her arm and gestured for the cigarette, so she handed it to him and he took a dramatic drag. Then he passed it back to me and I sent it around again, hoping it was true that you get mononucleosis only from kissing.

"Hey, have you heard the band yet?" Roxanne asked me.

"Yeah," I answered. "At the pep rally."

"Oh, that's *nothing*. Wait'll you hear. They've really got it."

As though on cue, the kids in the back of the bus began to work up a beat. First the drums, then a horn or two. They were playing a Beatle song. "It's been a hard day's night . . . dada da dada dadadum." Everybody knew the words. Everybody sang. And then another. "If I trust in you . . . da daaaaa, da da da dum. . . ." It was fun. I sang, too, for miles.

What started out a community sing amounted to an uproar as we neared Seth High. The captain of the cheerleaders started a chant:

"If you're for Urban, clap your hands!"

Everybody: *Clap clap*

"If you're for Urban, stamp your feet!"

Everybody: *Stamp stamp*

"If you're for Urban, jump *up!*"

Everybody jumped up. Then down. Then up and down.

"Hey we're *there!*" somebody shouted.

"There's Seth, over there."

The bus ruptured internally with screams of "Yaaaaaaay" and again "Yaaaaaaay." The drummer pounded wildly on his drums. The head cheerleader burst out of his seat yelling "BEAT SETH, BEAT SETH, BEAT SETH, BEAT SETH," and his followers took up the cry, yelling out the windows. When they disembarked they were still shrill-sounding "BEAT SETH, BEAT SETH" like the Zulus attacking an outpost, like the Gray hard-dying with the rebel yell. They rushed the stadium and then scattered over the section set aside for Urbanites. For most of them, the best part of the day was then over.

I found the stadium a startling sight. It was Lilliputian. The last football game I had seen was a professional one in an arena which was packed to the horizon with fifty or sixty thousand people. The college games I had seen on television were in equally huge, equally jammed stadiums. This stadium, with a wall not much higher than a back-yard fence, was not only tiny, it was also less than half filled. Where *was* everybody?

When I went to high school, local football games were an *event*. That of course was before television in most parts of the country. We who cherished our high school football teams hadn't ever sat in our living rooms watch-ing West Point play Annapolis, or the Packers play the Giants. We didn't know how silly were our little efforts compared to the Big League image on the screen. Hesitat-ing there at the entrance to Seth Field, I was glad I hadn't known. How slight would have been my pleasure. How great it really was.

Billy and Roxanne hesitated, too, at the stadium en-trance, but for a different reason. They had to size up the place and figure out the "in" spot. At least the pressing problem of where to sit in the stands hadn't changed. One still couldn't sit too far front (looks too eager), or too far back (might be missed), or too near rival gangs who might draw all the attention. One couldn't hesitate too long, either, or one might be caught hesitating, which would be almost as bad as sitting in the wrong place.

Billy saw three boys she knew and sat down with them. Roxanne and I sat with Angela and another girl to whom I was promptly introduced. Her name was Maureen. She was a tallish, tomboy type with long hair that waved too much to be go-go. I had never seen her before.

Kelly showed up panting. She had indeed been detained in gym and had made the last bus by seconds. We were then five in a row: Maureen, Angela, Roxanne, me, and Kelly. I made no offer to move from between the inseparable Beatle nuts because I wanted them to talk across me, which they did, primarily about Number 17 on the team—or was that him for sure?

"No, he's Number 28."

"No, Roxanne, that's him."

"Are you sure, Kelly, are you sure?"

"Sure, I can tell by his walk. That's him. That's him."

"Who's Billy sitting with?" I asked.

"George Polk, and he's an absolute ass," answered Roxanne.

"Walt is letting his hair grow," said Kelly about one of the cheerleaders. It was the ultimate compliment; Beatle nuts, as you may know, love anybody with hair.

"He's cute," I commented about Walt, who was.

"I just broke up with him," Roxanne sighed. "I went with him for a year."

"Gee, he's cute," I repeated. "Why did you break up?"

"He's really very immature," Roxanne said.

"How old is he?"

"Sixteen, but he acts very young."

"Oh."

"Boys our age are really very immature," noted Kelly.

"Gee, everybody broke up last summer," I said.

"Yes," said Roxanne. "Billy did too. She was going with Pete."

"Listen," said Roxanne, leaning close to me so she could whisper and still be heard over the frenzied cheerleaders. "Don't tell Gretel, but I have a date with Arnie Saturday night." (Note: Arnie is Gretel's ex.)

171

"Gee, do you?" I said. "I saw you talking to him at lunch."

"Yes. We've known each other a long time and it's nothing serious, but I hope Gretel won't be upset."

What did a girl's girl friend say when the girl's other girl friend told her such a thing? I didn't know.

Three rows in front of us sat Cooky and two friends. We never spoke, our row and theirs, never acknowledged each other's presence.

Billy, dragging a cute boy, crawled across us all and sat down next to Kelly. The boy, I found out, didn't count. He and Billy had a date the next night, true, but they were just friends.

"He's cute," I whispered to Roxanne.

"Yes, but he's very neurotic," she said.

"What do you mean?" I asked.

Roxanne answered, "Oh, he's very bright but he won't study or anything, won't even try. He's very rich. There are a lot of guys like him at Urban."

The girl cheerleaders performed the strange cheer I had witnessed at the pep rally—a kind of striptease frug—but I was the only one in the stands who noticed. When they finished, the boy cheerleaders jumped up and made hostile gestures toward their classmates, trying to get them to join in the cheering. They shouted something, too, but their words were lost over the second row. The band burst into victory tunes now and then, which probably meant we made occasional touchdowns, but I couldn't verify this, try as I might. Clearly, the point of being at Seth was the same as the point of eating lunch in one gulp: so you could look for boys and be seen by them. Nothing else mattered. Billy made several trips to the refreshment stand to check the whereabouts of various fellows. She brought back full reports and also pocketfuls of food which I thought was absolutely splendid.

172

Near the half, our attention was brought to the fact that somebody on our team was flat on the field. All action stopped as two boys on the bench got a stretcher and carried out the limp red-and-brown-clad body. The stands buzzed with "Who is it? Who is it?"

Roxanne reached across me and clutched Kelly's shoulder in a paroxysm of terror. "Is it him?" she gasped.

"No, it's Al," said Kelly.

"Thank God," said Roxanne, pulling back her arm.

"Is he dead?" asked a boy behind me.

"Naw," somebody answered. "Just broke his neck." Word bubbled up like water seeking its level: Al broke his neck. Is he dead? Naw. The head cheerleader got the news and turned to lead us all in three cheers for Al.

"Yay, Al. Yay, Al. Yay, Al," yelled his loyal fans.

One of the boys in the band started to play Taps on his trumpet but was quickly squelched by a teacher.

"Maybe he *is* dead," said the persistent fellow behind me.

"Nah," said his friend, sounding disappointed.

As the action on the field began again, Maureen suddenly became very agitated. She poked Angela and gestured hysterically toward the bleacher a section away from us. Angela gasped and poked Roxanne. She poked her again. And again. Then she pounded her on the arm.

"Roxanne, *look. A beard. Oh,* and he's *darling. Oh, Oh!*" Angela moaned, cried, whined, rasped, grabbing for her own forehead, her chest, her eyes; tearing at Roxanne's sweater, arm, knees.

"Where? Where?" cried Roxanne in Angela's pitch.

"There, there," wailed Angela, pointing with her pinky.

"Oh, my God," moaned Roxanne. "Oh, oh, oh. He's so *cute.* Oh, oh, oh. How completely tough. Kelly. Look. A *beard.*"

"Oh, oh, oh," groaned Kelly, poking Billy.

173

"Where, where?" panted Billy.

"They-er . . . right up they-er. Oh!" wept Kelly.

"Oh, my God," said Billy. But she didn't lose her cool. She narrowed her eyes and contemplated her next move.

Angela sneaked a look toward the bleachers. Then Roxanne sneaked a look. Then I did. What I saw six rows up and across an aisle was a young bearded face, not young enough to belong to a high school boy, but young —probably nineteen or so. The face rose above a deep green shaggy crew-necked sweater. With the boy with the beard was another boy about nineteen, slightly mangy but not bad-looking. The bearded one had a sharp, interesting profile.

When Kelly sneaked her second look she turned back pale and trembling. "He's lighting a cigarette," she reported, her voice husky with emotion.

"Oh my God, how sharp," said Roxanne. "How absolutely sharp."

Suddenly Billy materialized in the row behind us, stretched out like Madame Recamier on her chaise longue. I have no idea how she got there. She lit a cigarette and took long puffs of it, raising it into the sky after every inhale, and blowing smoke out in a long stream toward the cigarette from which it came.

"Hey, Billy, you're not allowed to smoke up here," Roxanne said. Billy gave her a small kick where she sat.

A few rows in front of the Beard, Seth's band beat out the rhythm for the cheerleaders' cry of "We want a *touch*down. We want a *touch*down. We want a *touch*down." Then "Yaaaaaaay," screamed the crowd, as the touchdown was made, and "MAKE THAT POINT. MAKE THAT POINT. MAKE THAT POINT" became the chant.

For the first time that afternoon, our gang seemed to

174

know what was happening on the football field. They leaped to their feet, jumped up on the benches they had been sitting on, balanced on their toes, sprang up and down, and screamed vowel sounds. The Beard could see them now all right, all right. Not wanting to appear odd, I jumped into the excitement, and followed my friends as they pulled at each other's sweater sleeves and pounded each other on the arms and back. When they screamed hooray, I screamed hooray. I knew a secret, however. I knew that it wasn't our team that had scored.

When we sat down, Roxanne peeked to make sure all that activity hadn't been in vain. She delivered the message: the Beard was still there.

"He looks like Jesus," said Angela.

"Oh he does, he does," squealed Roxanne. "Oh Saviour, save me, save me." Everybody giggled.

She said it again, only more dramatically, from a semi-kneeling position.

"Oh *stop* that," giggled Kelly. "You're awful."

Angela jumped up and announced that the football game was too much for her. She wanted to be alone, she said, and she crawled onto the bench in front of us. Maureen said it was all too much for her, too, and followed Angela. That left empty spaces on our bench that had to be adjusted, so we all took new positions: Roxanne sliding to the left, Kelly crossing over her, I squeezing between them. Roxanne was appointed to find out where the Beard was now. She indicated by means of head motions that he was still there.

Angela turned around looking strangely desperate.

Roxanne asked her what was wrong. She whispered, "I have to *go*."

"Oh *God*," said Roxanne. "Not *now*."

"Me, too," said Kelly.

I said, "Me, too," too.

"Where is it?" Kelly mouthed to Angela. Angela didn't know.

"You can't go *now*," Roxanne said.

"I have to. My teeth are floating," Kelly said.

Roxanne laughed. Having to go so badly that something or other was floating or about to be flooded was a major source of humor for my classmates. I had heard a wide variety of graphic descriptions of the need "to go," especially at lunch. One description which caused a universal outburst of laughter was "If I don't pee, you'd better build an ark." The laughter was primed, everytime it died down, with "Listen, I'm not kidding." I heard so much of this particular brand of chatter, in fact, that I had stopped hearing it. I heard it again at the football game because there the subject of going to the john was fraught with problems.

For one thing, no one knew where "it" was, and no one would ask. For another, in order to get to the exit from where a john might be seen, we had to walk past Seth's band "and all those guys." I could not volunteer to lead the way, of course, though I was tempted to do so just to get the subject changed.

In time we decided that we would run for the exit as soon as something happened on the football field that would draw attention away from us. We did just that when Angela gave the signal. Then we stopped and giggled, not knowing what to do next.

"It must be over there," said Angela.

"No, I don't think so," said Kelly.

"But what'll we *do?*" tittered Angela.

"Listen, I've got to *go*," said Kelly. "Be serious. Ask that girl."

Angela tiptoed across the exit and whispered in a girl's ear, then looked back at us hopelessly. The girl didn't know either.

"Ask that man at the gate," Angela said to Kelly.

Kelly cringed against the wall. "Are you *kidding?*" she gasped.

Whereupon Angela stamped her foot, tossed her head theatrically, charged over to the uniformed man at the gate, and boldly inquired, "Where is the ladies' room, please?" Then she came back and, without looking at us, led us to the john.

As she went through the door, she let out a little shout of joy. "Hey, there's a *huge* mirror in here," she said. Whereupon she and Kelly immediately forgot about their floating teeth. They placed combs, brushes, and all their makeup on a window ledge and peered at themselves in the mirror, saying, "Oh, my God, I look *awful*" and "Oh, look at my *hair*" and "Why didn't you *tell* me . . . I have dirt on my cheek."

I left them for a booth at the back of the room. When I returned I had one of the worst moments of this entire adventure. As I write it down, it seems so ludicrous, I can't believe I actually responded to it. But I did.

Kelly was off to the side fixing her eyebrows and was, for the moment, out of the picture. Angela had taken down her hair and was looking at it in the mirror. She appeared to be concentrating so hard I didn't want to disturb her, so I just quietly removed my sunglasses and the bow I had clipped above my bangs, and started combing my hair. Suddenly I felt her staring at me. I saw, in the mirror, that she had turned toward me, the better to scrutinize my face. She thus blocked my exit, though that was not her intention. She could not know, after all, that my impulse was to flee.

"How old are you?" she asked, her eyes on my face.

I turned away from her and fussed in my pocketbook. When I got my head down so I wouldn't meet her eyes, I mumbled "Sixteen and a half."

"You look *much* older," she said. "I suppose everybody tells you that."

177

I tried to smile while I said that, yes, they did; but I felt so sick to my stomach I could barely open my mouth at all.

"You look nineteen or twenty," Angela continued, watching me in the mirror.

I was clammy.

"Gosh, here I am trying to look older and you don't even have to try. I wish *I* looked older. What is it about you, I wonder."

She stepped closer.

Kelly, who hadn't heard Angela's comments, turned to us just then. "What are you doing, Angela? Come on, stop standing there loving yourself. Go to the john so we can leave this hole." Angela shrugged and followed orders. I quickly put on my sunglasses and hair bow. I longed to get back to the stands where I could fade into the crowd, but we had to wait until there was a forward pass and the band began to watch the field instead of us—which it was not doing anyway. I wished it would rain and we could go home. I wished there were any way at all I could get out of that stadium before Angela started telling all the other girls how old I looked and wasn't that interesting.

It didn't rain and I couldn't escape, but the Beard saved me. He did something which was so unexpected, and so against rules of the Game, that I could only assume the gods had had a hand in it. He came alive. From across the stands he waved to Angela and Maureen, and gestured for them to sit with him. He moved, breathed, and smiled. He was *real.*

The girls went into shock. They hadn't wanted him to be real. He was just for fun. They tightened like wild animals sensing a fire. The Beard stood up and moved closer to our benches. Roxanne reached across me and gripped Kelly's arm. Suddenly a note sailed into our midst. It landed at Kelly's feet but she wouldn't pick it up.

Roxanne and Kelly drew their feet away from the note and stared at it in horror. Angela picked it up, opened it, and slowly read it aloud. It said, "We'll give you a ride home. Wait for us."

Nobody looked now at the boy with the beard. Nobody cheered now for the valiant men on the football field. No longer were my friends gay ballerinas doing delirious entrechats on the bench tops. Now they were a Greek chorus voicing dread and doom. "He wants to take us home," they repeated, as though it were "The ship is sunk, the men are drowned."

One by one, shadowy and stealthily, those who had strayed rose and returned to home bench, and then there were again six of us in a row, and not a sound.

The Game was over. So was the football game, and we lost that, too. By the time we got to the bottom of the bleachers, the Beard was there. He and his friend stood in front of Angela and Maureen, blocking their way. The rest of us cowered behind them. They talked to Angela and she to them. Then she turned to us and said she had informed them that they had to take all or nobody and they agreed to take all.

Billy said, "No, Angela, come on, we'll take the bus." But Angela and Maureen were off with the boys, leaving us to follow, which we did, shaking our heads and mumbling that we wanted to take the bus. We marched for blocks, passing bus stops as we went. As we rushed along, Billy and Kelly began to think it was all very funny. When we got to the car they went wild.

"We're not going to get in *that!*" screamed Billy.

"You guys are *kidding!*" shouted Kelly.

There proceeded a loud argument, punctuated by loud laughter, about whether or not we were going to get in the car.

*They* laughed. I couldn't, because if I relaxed the

179

muscles in my face I would have twitched. The car looked like a prop from a movie called *I Was a Teenage Wreck*. All the paint had been rubbed or burned off of it, all the chrome had been stripped off, a fender was missing, and the hood was tied on with heavy cord. Or maybe it was the motor that was tied on. Anyway, there was a knotted rope around the entire front of the car.

I believe that, despite their laughter, my companions were as afraid to get in that car as I was. If they weren't when they saw the outside of it, they were when they saw the inside. The car was a coupé of some early postwar vintage, meaning its back seat was big enough for two adults and a deer mouse. There was no upholstery on the seats and the springs had popped through in at least four places. Where the floor should have been was a pile of dirty laundry. The roof was bare steel.

The girls were laughing hysterically over the fact that the boys thought we were all going to fit in the car with our books, sweaters, bags of peanuts and half-eaten candy bars. But meanwhile they were backing away, and I think they would have turned and run, except that Angela yanked open the door and shoved Maureen into the back seat. There was no getting away after that. Billy climbed in next to Maureen, I squeezed into the right-hand corner, Roxanne and Kelly sat on our three laps, and the books, sweaters, and other impedimenta were distributed over the top of us—all to the sound of *ha-ha* and *yeeeow* and *eeeeeee*. Angela sat up front between the beardless boy, who drove, and the Beard, who had one arm around Angela and the other out the window to keep the door from flying open.

"ROXANNE, MOVE YOUR ASS TO THE LEFT, WILL YOU? YOU'RE BREAKING MY LEG!" shouted Billy.

"I CAN'T BREATHE!" screamed Maureen.

180

"LET ME OUT!" howled Roxanne.

And we were off on the twenty-mile trip home, if indeed that's where we were being taken.

I have never been so scared in my life. By the time the car was in third gear it was going sixty miles an hour. And traffic was heavy. The boy at the wheel knew a lot of people in the other cars on the road, and he wanted to wave to them. When he couldn't catch them on the left, he passed them on the right. Occasionally he waved with both hands. When he did put his hands on the wheel, he left his head out the window, so he could exchange pleasantries with other drivers and their passengers. My friends thought he was a "Rye-it."

*"Eeeeeeek! Watch out! Yippee! Ha-ha-ha!"*

Very funny. Obviously, we were all going to get killed. I could picture the wreckage clearly. At least when *their* bodies were found, somebody would be able to identify them. I was carrying identification for a high school junior who didn't exist. No one on earth knew where I was. If our accident made the papers, Bess might eventually get the idea that maybe *that's* where I had gone. On the other hand, she might pretend she had never heard of me, which would be the wiser course. And I couldn't even write a last letter to Frank because someone was sitting on my hands.

The seven other people in the car were having a marvelous, normal time getting acquainted. They wouldn't have sounded any different if they had been at a dance in the gym.

"Hi. I'm Billy and this is Maureen, Kelly, Roxanne, and Lyn. Angela you already know. And what are *your* names?"

"I'm Beard and that's Junk."

"Hi."

"Hi."

181

"Hi."

"Hi."

"Where are you birds from? You at Urban?" asked Junk.

"Yes, we're all juniors. Where're you guys from?"

"We used to go to Urban."

"Gee, did you?"

"Yeah."

"What were you doing at the football game?"

No answer.

"Goddam it, Roxanne, look out for my foot, will you? Shit. Move your elbow on *that* side," said Billy.

"Hey, Junk," said Beard. "You know who the one with the shades looks like? Slink. Yeah, Slink. Hey, Shades, you know who you look like? Slink."

"Who's she?" asked Roxanne, the one with the shades. Laughter from boys. "Don't you know who Slink is?"

"Unh-unh," said Roxanne.

More laughter from the boys.

"Christ, get off my kidneys, they're floatin'," said Billy. *"Billy, you're awful,"* said Kelly.

"Well, they are. They're floatin'." And so on, about floods and things.

"Lyn's not talking at all," observed Maureen. "Hey, Lyn, you scared?" she shouted from her corner.

"Lyn's a quiet one," said Roxanne.

You'd be quiet, too, I thought, if you were old enough to know you were about to be dead. You'd be quiet, too, if Angela thought you looked old and you were old enough to know how old you were.

I went on talking to them, for miles, but in my head: "What are you doing in this wreck with those two dirty old boys?" I hollered. "Don't you know why they were at that football game? They were there to pick up sweet young girls, you dumb kids, you. Why don't you grow up?"

182

Beard and Angela were whispering. But I heard them anyway. He said, "Hey, you got big eyes, you know that?" She said, "No I don't." He said, "Yeah, you do. Big eyes."

And we careened madly on, Billy having to pee as it were, and Maureen getting her ribs bashed, Kelly hitting her head on the roof every time the car jumped a puddle, and I—pained both physically and mentally—softly praying in my corner. (There are no atheists in hot rods, either.)

"So this is what American teenagers are really like," said Maureen. Everybody broke up.

Well, we didn't get killed and we weren't sold into white slavery and they did take us back to the city. We decided on Urban as the most central drop-off point, and that, by heaven, with a screech of brakes is where we wound up. Beard took his arm off the door and it flew open. He and Angela stepped out. The front seat went down, and the rest of us untangled onto the street. The boys drove away leaving us stamping around, waving arms and legs to get blood back in circulation, hollering "Wow, what a relief and *God, that was something* and *Christ, my arm's broken.*" When the exercises were over, Kelly asked Roxanne and Billy to her house for dinner with "Nobody's home, let's make spaghetti," Angela and Maureen waved goodbye and started up the hill, and I stood still, waiting for the shock to wear off.

Oh yes, I forgot to mention, Angela made a date to meet Beard in front of a movie theater at 10 P.M. I don't know if she kept it, and I'm not sure I'd tell if I did. One thing I did know, though, was that Kelly was a woman of her word. She had said we'd get home somehow or other, and we did.

# 17

THE FOOTBALL GAME with David was a different sort of occasion. It was a night game, for one thing. Our elders knew where it was, for a second thing. And I knew how we were going to get there and back, for a third thing, because Bess, bless her heart, had granted me the use of her car. For a fourth thing, I could be comfortable with David because he knew my secret. I could even laugh in front of him without worrying that the sound would shock him into calling the FBI.

My date with him was the first I'd had with a fifteen-and-a-half-year-old since I was fourteen, but I must say I doubt that it had taken me so long to get ready the last time. First I had to clean the four coats of paint I wore to school off my face, then I had to reapply them. After that I had to work on some eye makeup, but very cautiously; I didn't want to look too sophisticated, after all. And then Bess had me trying on combinations and permutations of my wardrobe for about a half hour until she approved of a brown turtleneck stretch top, a tan skirt, a fuzzy beige sweater, and my new heels. I had wanted to wear the Pappagallos because those $8.95 heels were wearing out at a fearful speed, but she said no, not right for a Friday night date. Just not right.

"Why don't you tease your hair a bit?" she suggested. "On the crown, behind your bangs. Yes, that's better. Very cute. Gives you a little height."

"Doesn't it look older?" I asked.

"No," she said. "It doesn't, really. Looks very good. I think you ought to wear it that way all the time."

"Do you see any gray yet?" I asked her.

"No, nothing. But if you're worried about it, we can give you a touch-up next week."

I told her I thought we'd better, and she nodded.

"Are you going to wear your glasses?" she said, sounding disapproving.

I nodded and put them on.

"But it'll be dark at the game. Why do you need them?"

"Too risky," I told her. "There might be bright lights at the game, or we might go somewhere for something to eat. Much too risky."

"But you might meet somebody interesting," she said.

"That's the point," I replied. And then my date arrived, right on time. His parents brought him. He was wearing cotton slacks and a flannel shirt and his zippered jacket. He appeared, thank God, not the least self-conscious. He was smiling quite warmly. In fact, he was grinning.

"Hi," he said. "You ready?"

"Ready," I answered.

"My mother's out in the car. So's my dad. They want to see you before we go."

Bess asked why they didn't come in. David, unzipping his jacket four inches and zipping it two, said they only had a minute. So we all went out to the car.

His mother was in the driver's seat, his father beside her.

"All ready?" she asked merrily.

185

"All ready," I said.

Bess leaned on the car window. "Doesn't she look cute?" she asked. "Check the shoes."

David's mother looked me over. "Perfect," she said. "God, that *outfit*. From the back you look twelve."

I smiled.

"Keep it clean, now," said David's dad.

"I will," I answered merrily.

"Don't be too late," said Mrs. Bodine.

"We won't," I said merrily. "We'll be home right after the game."

"Listen," she said, less merrily. "You've driven Bess's car before, haven't you?"

"Of course," I answered, kicking Bess lightly in the ankle in case she had an impulse to tell the truth.

"Let's *go*," said David, and so we did. But I couldn't resist leaving a parting message that went "Don't *worry*, I've been driving since I was sixteen."

As soon as David set me on course he began talking about how much he hated having to be chauffeured. "I'm practically the only guy in the whole school who doesn't have a car, except for the guys in tenth grade." His whole life would change the day he could drive, he said, staring out the window. He knew how to drive, of course, but he was too young even to get a permit. He *couldn't wait* to get his permit, and, boy, just as soon as he got it he'd earn the money to buy himself a car, and he knew where to get a used one for fifty dollars that hardly needed any work and would be just great. "Most of the guys get new cars when they're sixteen, but my dad thinks I should buy my own. I don't care what it is as long as it runs. . . . Turn left at the next light. . . . How's it going at Urban?"

"Great," I said.

"Have they found you out yet?"

186

I shook my head.

"Boy, I don't get that," he said.

I told him about the day I had the physical and the narrow escape at the eye chart. He was so awed he refused to believe me. "You've gotta show me that chart," he said. I told him he could go to Urban and see it any time he wanted. He replied that he wouldn't go to Urban if I paid him.

"Did you get out of that dumb study hall yet?" he asked.

When I said no he shook his head disgustedly. "I thought you were going to switch to geometry. What happened to that?"

"I can't take geometry," I said. "Even with your help, I'd flunk."

"You would not."

"I would so," I insisted. "I don't even remember any of the axioms."

"What's an axiom?"

"Gee, I don't know. I can't remember any. Yes, 'two things equal to the same thing are equal to each other.' That's an axiom."

"No, that's an assumption."

"An assumption? What's an assumption?"

"Two things equal to the same thing are equal to each other. That's an assumption. I remember now. Old Mac-Intosh told us when he handed out the books: there used to be axioms before the Space Age. They don't have them anymore. They're assumptions."

"You see what I mean?" I said. "I'd flunk."

David didn't understand why I was so worried about flunking. "What are you going to do? Try to go to college next?" he asked.

I laughed.

"All I know," he said, "is that you must be bored stiff. I

187

don't know how you live through a day with those boring courses. . . . Turn right at the next light and go up the hill into the parking lot. Park at the end. That's for visitors. I hope the school's still open. What time is it?"

It was seven o'clock. The sun was just setting on David's high school, reflecting pink off its glass and steel and off the flecks of mica in its rough-cut rocks.

There was nothing around it for miles. Nothing but soft hills and shaggy trees and fresh, clean air. It stood where the hills rolled flat out into a valley, a U-shaped, two-story structure with a stately stone entranceway and manicured evergreens terraced at its base. I called it Super High.

All the classrooms were entered from the outdoors by way of roofed-over, locker-lined ramps. In cold weather, the ramps were heated. The administrative offices were the only rooms entered from indoor hallways, and those were flooded with light, and glass-enclosed. There was none of the brownness of Urban. The classroom walls were painted pale green or yellow, the floors were tan and black tile, the wastebaskets were pastel-colored.

As I walked around with David I was deeply grateful I had not tried to enroll in a school like Super. I would have looked like a black beetle in those sparkling halls, like a woolly bug on the yellow countertops of my kitchen just after they're waxed.

And the kids who were roaming the halls, welcoming visitors. So beautiful. All of them tall and tanned and smiling. All, fresh and crisp and clean. And poised. So poised. A couple of them smiled blindingly at David, bidding him "Hi." When they did, I walked behind him, trying to hide in his shadow.

One boy guide handed me a copy of Super's newspaper. A girl gave me a souvenir booklet containing the school song and funny couplets delineating what was expected of Super girls: neat hairdos, not bouffant, and not up in rollers; modest makeup; simple jewelry; no club jackets, pins, or sweatshirts outside of meetings; no sheer blouses; no slit shifts; no stretch pants, skirts to the bend of the knee; stockings with closed shoes, no sandals; and a bold-face reminder—no smoking on the school grounds.

Then we went outside to the cafeteria. Outside, yet. It was a huge covered patio protected in cold weather by walls of warm air, and on it were enough picnic-style tables and benches to seat an army or two. The tables were usually filled during the morning coffee break, David said, but during lunch you could eat anywhere you wanted and most of the kids sat out on the mall sort of picnicking until midwinter.

There was very little to say about Super beyond "Wow." Its acres of campus were magnificently land-scaped, its parking lots were twice the size needed either by its teachers for their station wagons, or by its students for their sports cars. It was the ideal. It was functioning perfection. It was tomorrow. And I suppose somebody said that about Urban forty-odd years ago, too, but that's the risk you take when you play with axioms.

The football stadium conformed to Super standards. The top of it was level with the parking lot and entrance; to get to the rows of seats you walked downward toward the field. The stadium itself was easily four times the size of the one I had visited at Seth, and it was floodlighted in a way that made the field look as if it stood in the noonday sun. I didn't remember ever seeing a high school field equipped for night games before, but I refrained from telling this to David, who already suspected I was a walking mummy. Anyway, our lines of communication were temporarily severed. While we were standing on line for tickets, he had seen several of his teachers and couldn't stop marveling over them. Whatever his reactions meant, they were all his. I didn't understand any of them.

He kept muttering, "Old MacIntosh. Boy, did you see

189

that? He's my geometry teacher. I wonder if he saw me. Old Mac. Boy."

And "Oh, cheez, there's my history teacher. Old Kendall. What's *he* doing here? Cheez, I think he sees us."

"Old Kendall," about twenty-seven years old, passed within a foot of us, reached out, patted my date on his shoulder, and said, "Hello there, David," and I thought he was lost forever. But he spoke, so I was reassured. He said, "Cheez, did you see him? That was my history teacher. What's he doing here anyway?"

We sat in the top row of the stands, at David's request, so we could make a quick getaway. "We don't have to stay the whole game, do we?" he had asked. "It'll be a real bore. Nobody'll be there. You just look around, then we'll C.O.D." (Cut Out Directly, he said that meant.)

A girl standing behind us tapped David on the shoulder. "Hi, David," she said.

He turned around. "Hi, Phyllis," he said.

"What're you doing here? I thought you hated football."

"Yeah, I do," he said, blushing. "She wanted to see the school. She's from Urban." He introduced us by first names: "This is Lyn, this is Phyllis." She was cute. Short, a little full-blown, brown-haired.

"Oh, Urban. Gee. Do you know Georgia Katz?"

"Unh-unh," I said. "I'm new there and I haven't met anybody yet." (No sense in getting involved, I decided.)

"Oh. Well, if you meet her, tell her hi. I met her at Jeff Link's party. Boy, that was a crazy party. Right, David?" She poked him.

"Yeah," he said.

"Hey, who'd you get for geometry?" she asked him.

"MacIntosh," he answered.

"Lucky *you*," she squealed. "Guess who I got."

"Who?"

"Guess."

"Trilby."

"Yes!" she shrieked.

David rolled his eyes and feigned a stomach blow. "Ugh," he said. "She's the worst. I mean, she's a good teacher, but she's the worst. Wicked."

Phyllis laughed and poked David, doing an imitation of wicked Trilby in which he joined. Then they laughed together.

The players ran out on the field below and Phyllis shrieked. "Oh, I've got to go. I'm with Linda and Corby—down there, see? Are you going to Y.D. tomorrow?"

"Don't know," David said. "Maybe."

"Well, if you are, I'll see ya. Okay?"

"Okay."

We waved so-long and she dashed away.

"Boy, she's wasted," said David as soon as she was out of sight.

"What do you mean?" I asked.

"She's a waste; a mess from head to toe. *Wasted.*"

I had thought he liked her.

Super's band, about twice the size of Urban's and much more splendidly uniformed, began to play and the game got under way. Next to the band there were about fifty blond boys and girls in white shirts cheering madly and forming words out of flash cards. That was the Pep Club, David said. They were very active.

I told David I'd never seen as many blonds in one place as I'd seen in his school and thought it was terribly interesting. "Do you suppose being rich makes you blond?" I asked.

"Boy, are you stupid," he said. "That's not *real* blond hair."

"Even on the boys?"

"Sure," he said.

The cheerleaders, all girls, had on white pleated skirts and heavy letter-sweaters. They carried gold megaphones. ("The school colors are white and gold. I think that's neat, don't you?") And they were very active, David said. It was really something to become a cheerleader at Super.

"You see that girl in the middle? She's the head cheerleader. Didi Thomas. And she's only a junior. She's the smartest kid in the school, I think. Boy, what a brain. She's an honor student. And editor of the paper. And vicepresident of the class. She'll probably get the lead in the junior class play, too, cause it's a musical and boy, can she sing. She's a soloist in the Glee Club. Last year she was Miss May Day and boy, she looked *great*. She sang at the prom, too. I know her from the Young Democrats Club. She's the treasurer. She's in my chem class, too. What a brain. She's going to be a nuclear physicist—"

"Are you putting me on?" I interrupted.

"What do you mean?"

"Are you kidding me?"

David looked offended. "I don't know what you mean. Where's the joke?" he said.

"Never mind, I'm sorry," I said. "Go on."

"That's all. Except she's in Student Service, too. If you had gone to my school instead of that ugly old bomb you're in, you probably would have had her as a guide and then you really would have learned something."

The game went on, Super in the lead, without David's seeing anyone else he knew. He watched the action with what could easily pass for real interest, but about every other play he asked if I was ready to leave.

"At the half," I said. "I want to see what your band does out on the field."

"Okay. They're pretty good. And you'll see the drill team, too."

192

"What's that?" I asked.

"You'll see," he said. And indeed I did.

We got up at the half and stood behind our seats where Phyllis had been standing. We had a wonderful view of the field below us, and I enjoyed the sight of the band going through snappy maneuvers in their white-and-gold uniforms. Toy soldiers molded from vanilla ice cream. Candy soldiers in Barton's window.

Then an excited voice on a loudspeaker announced that the newly formed girls' drill team, all one hundred members, were about to perform, for the first time this year, out on the field. "I know you'll all enjoy them," the announcer shouted. "And here they come."

To the sound of loud cheers and applause, one hundred girls in short-skirted uniforms and ankle-high white boots assembled in the center of the field. Every light that wasn't directly on them was turned off. In the white-light of the spots, they formed a phalanx. Then they began to move—*snap, snap, click, click,* in precision—forming lines and figures and numbers and letters. Not a girl was under five feet seven. Not one could have weighed more than 115 pounds. Each had blond hair falling straight to the shoulders. Each was golden bronze, or, at least, made up to look that way. Collectively, they were magnificent.

For their last drill they formed a line straight across the field from goal to goal. Their backs were to us at first; they marched in place facing the visitors' side. Then they whirled around to face their own side of the stands and began a slow march in perfect step, in perfect rhythm with the drums in the band. Right at us they came, one hundred strong, arms up, hands on each other's shoulders, the spotlights widening on them as they marched closer and closer. I was sure they were going to keep right on marching, right over the top of us all, right on, out into the night.

And I felt that they should. The super-youth, the finished products of our superabundance and our superstrength. It's their world now, I thought. It really is. We have given it to them for better or worse. They are more than we were and better than we were. We created these super-people and now we can do nothing but wish them well. Good luck to you, golden girls, I said under my breath. And while they were still marching at me, I tapped David's arm and whispered, "Let's go."

# 18

THERE WAS MORE to my date with David.

After the game we went for a soda, and when we'd finished, the nice, chatty waitress handed *me* the check. How did she know I was the one with the money?

Then I flooded the car trying to start it in the parking lot, and it played dead while David and I panicked about being late and having to explain to his parents. For a moment we thought we were going to have to call them, but David gallantly decided to take the wheel and see what he could do to save us. While I waited on the sidewalk, he started the car and got it, jerking and bucking at too high a speed, to the street. "Don't tell Bess," he said, shaking. "I've never driven alone before."

"You were great," I told him, and he was pleased.

When I pulled up to the curb in front of his house, he opened the door, put his foot out of the car, and then stopped. He pulled his foot in and shut the door.

"Listen," he said. "You want to go to a party next Saturday?"

"Yes," I said.

"I've got to warn you, I don't know what kind of a party it's going to be."

"What do you mean?" I asked, for about the twentieth time that night.

"Well, it might be square. I don't know who's going to be there. They're not all from Super. These are a bunch of kids who went to Europe together last summer."

"Did you go with them?" I asked.

"Yeah, with this student group," he answered.

"Gee, you never mentioned it. Did you have a good time?"

"Oh, not bad. It was kind of boring after a while. Anyway, there's going to be a reunion at this girl's house on Saturday. I wasn't going to go, but if you want to go, I'll take you. It might be very boring. I mean, you shouldn't get the idea that all teenage parties are like this one."

"I won't," I said. "Honest. I'd love to go."

"Okay," he said. "Now, when we get there, we'll flake off. You pick up some guys, do anything you want to. We'll just go together; we won't hang around together. Okay?"

"Okay," I said.

"And listen, there might be some making out, too, I don't know."

"What's that mean?" I asked.

"That's anything," he said.

"Necking?"

"Yeah, that."

"More than necking?"

"Yeah, it can be."

"Going all the way?"

"Yeah."

"Do many kids do that? Go all the way?"

He looked at me and shrugged with resignation. "I knew you would ask me that," he said. "I just knew it."

"Well, what's the answer?"

David shrugged again. "A lot of guys talk a lot, but I don't think many guys do. Some guys have had a quick butt, I guess. At least they say they have."

"What's a quick butt?"

"Boy," said David, shaking his head. "I don't know if you're as dumb as you sound or if you're just square. 'What's a quick butt?' A quick butt's a quick butt, that's what it is."

"Okay," I said. "No more questions."

I thanked him for taking me to the football game and he shrugged. "I'll call you," he said. Then he went over again the directions he had given me for getting back to Bess's, got out of the car, shut the door, and leaned down on the rim of the open window.

"You know," he said pensively, "I'm going to do this in about ten years. I'm going to go back to school and pass for a junior. I could get away with it because I have a young face."

"Bye, David," I said, putting the car in drive.

He waved and went in his house.

# 19

DAVID's got a crush on you."

That's what Bess insisted the morning after my date with the lad, and went on insisting for the duration of my stay with her. Having somebody think a fifteen-and-a-half-year-old fellow has a crush on her is not the sort of thing a lady labeled past her prime by the rest of the world finds offensive, so I didn't argue.

Bess based her statement on the fact that David telephoned nearly every evening and twice on Saturdays. He called to find out what I was doing and how I was getting away with doing it. I believe that he was hoping, each time he called, that Bess would tell him I was in jail. Clearly, every day I passed successfully he lost another pound of faith in Urban's school system. "How'd you do today?" he would ask, and I'd tell him about homework, quizzes, problems, and specific events that had amused me. He'd chuckle now and then, but what he really wanted to know was what I thought of my teachers, my courses, my high school. I would not tell him, then, in the midst of his learning and the midst of his concern. I can tell him now.

This chapter, then, is for David. Some of it he already knows. Most of it, he doesn't.

Mr. Goodman, the American history teacher I had initially found tranquilizing, had, after the first week, the same effect on me that he had on the rest of the class. Numbing. Perish the word, boring. There was absolutely no reason to stay awake in his class oftener than the once a week he asked questions. If you were clever, you would only have to stay awake every other week; you could quickly figure out his pattern of soliciting answers from individual members of the class, and play the odds against your getting called on during what he termed "an oral quiz."

Precisely as Mr. Goodman had said he would conduct the class, he conducted it. During the first five minutes he took the roll, giving a black mark to anyone who was not silent while he did so. Then he lectured on the nine or ten pages of text we had been assigned to read the night before. He did not expand on the text in any way; he went over it heading by heading, outlining on the board as he went (Printing Press, A, B; Fur Trade, A, B, C; Religious Freedom, A; etc.). If time remained after he finished, the class was supposed to start reading the next ten pages of text, which were, in any case, that night's homework. But this was the time my classmates got most of their homework done for their afternoon classes. Or read fan magazines.

At no time in the period were the pupils encouraged to ask questions about either the text or the lecture. That might have been because he knew they wouldn't ask any anyway. Unsolicited discussions and questions were frowned on in all the classes I attended at Urban. A raised hand in any of those classes signaled a neurotic on the loose and was as likely to get lopped off as recognized.

Even I came to think that anyone who volunteered questions, answers, or general information was crazy. In the one class in which I saw hands raised unexpectedly (English), the two boys who raised them were immediately ordered to the first seats of the last row. There they could be quickly identified as troublemakers, and kept from spreading their poison.

When we were assigned written homework in history, we were given at least a week to prepare it. The assignment never varied from: "Answer the questions at the end of the chapter under 'Text Study Guide.'" The questions thereunder were rephrased subheads from the body of the chapter, and amounted to a test of the student's reading comprehension and ability to follow directions. For instance, the first chapter in the book, fifty-two pages long, covered the colonization of America. The questions at the end were as follows:

1. Give four reasons for the Age of Discovery and explain each.
2. What improvements were brought by Spain to the New World? List as many as you can.
3. What were the main ideas of mercantilism, especially as applied to the colonies?
4. Compare the power of churches in the Spanish, French, and English colonies.
5. Why did the Spanish and French colonies in America have limited success? What was the reason for the greater success of the English colonies? List the reasons in three parallel columns.
6. Why was the defeat of the Spanish Armada important?
7. Give as many reasons as you can for the establishment of the English colonies. Tell why settlers went to them. List the names of the thirteen colonies. (See map, p. 40.)

8. Study the diagram on p. 25, then describe the three triangular trade routes.

9. After studying the diagrammatic map on p. 48, list the major products of the southern, middle, and New England colonies.

10. Describe the various social classes and groups in colonial America. Which ones found in Europe were missing?

To answer these, one had to write out all the italicized sentences, lists, and enumerated statements in the chapter, to say nothing of whole paragraphs, verbatim. And I, for one, found scripting the answers to such all-encompassing "questions" tedious, irritating, and thoroughly unenlightening. I did get my homework done on time, and I did it as instructed. I don't know if I did it correctly because I never got any of it back. I do know, however, that without referring to my notes, I could not now answer the ten questions above any better than could anyone else who was in my history class or, I'll wager, any one of you who just read through them.

I did enjoy reading my history book, though my particular pleasure could not possibly have been shared by my classmates. I enjoyed the book because, despite a 95 average, I didn't learn American history the first time I studied it.

I have come, since, both to appreciate the subject and to deplore my lack of knowledge of it. Therefore I was enchanted to have to read about Columbus dying a pauper (did you know that?); and the Spaniards giving us such words as canyon, corral, and mosquito; and Roger Williams insisting that the land on which the colonists had settled really belonged to the Indians.

But nothing could dispel the fascination quicker than Mr. Goodman's canned lectures, mechanical outlines, and routinized quizzes. I believe I understand the problems he had, trying to cover the whole of American history in one year. I know, too, that he was genuinely concerned that his class learn what was necessary for college entrance exams. He would often say, "You'd better worry about the marks you get here and now, so you can have the best possible opportunities when you get out."

I am nonetheless intolerant. I believe that American history as taught to me seventeen years ago was a damn dull subject. The way it was taught to me then was precisely the way it was taught by Mr. Goodman of Urban High. The way it was taught to me then, I discovered, was the same damn dull way it was taught by David's teacher at Super High. And I sincerely hope that somewhere in this country there is a U. S. 1 teacher whose class is able to stay awake at least three days a week. Mine wasn't.

In the Spanish quiz on which I cheated I got what I deserved: a failing grade—50, to be exact. In the next quiz I got an 80, and that with mighty effort and Bess's tutoring. By some miracle, I got an A— in the recitation of *"Treinta días tiene septiembre . . ."* but then, B was the lowest grade given out on that one. Miss Zorri thought we all had very good pronunciation, and that's what she graded recitations on.

We had no written homework in Spanish at all. Nor did we use our textbooks. Despite this (or because of it?), and despite the constant presence of borderline hysteria, there was a very high level of interest in Spanish on the part of everyone in the class, including the rowdies. In time, their misbehavior took the form of early morning heckling and occasional outbursts of laughter or conversation. One such occurred, for instance, when Mickey was finally dispatched to the principal's office for a reprimanding. He returned to his friends a hero, full of stories about how he put down the principal and escaped undaunted. The hour in which he left and returned, and the following day's period, were lost to us all.

The young lady in front of me turned out to be a veritable genius, and I poked her on the shoulder frequently for help. She gave it, sighing, for after all, I was a low eleven. Dependent, yes, but her superior.

The reason I was having so much trouble learning Spanish (and I have come away able to say only *Buenos días* and *treinta días tiene* you know what) was that I had never learned a language by ear before. The two languages I have studied were taught to me in the old visual fashion. I learned them by reading them and watching words being written on a blackboard. Apparently, I am rigidly unable to adjust to any other method. Whenever Miss Zorri spoke to us in Spanish, I wanted to know how she spelled what she was saying. When she said "*¿Cómo está?*" to the class, and we were supposed to be answering "*Bien, gracias. ¿Y usted?*" I was hung up trying to visualize "*¿Cómo está?*" I wanted to know if it was "*¿Comó esta?*" or "*¿Co mestá?*" or "*¿Com'esta?*" And while I was busily searching for the expression in my textbook, the class went merrily on to *dispénseme usted, lo siento,* and *ha sido usted muy amable.*

But my accent was very good because I spent a lot of time with Xavier Cugat records in my youth. And anyway, it's never too late to find out in what areas of life one is a blockhead.

An education of some variety was often more accessible in the halls of Urban than in its classrooms. I cherished, particularly, the times I met Gretel unexpectedly and had a chance to lope at her side as she dashed in and out of between-class amenities. There was the time, for example, that we collided with Billy on our way to English class. She grabbed Gretel by the arm.

"Gretel," she gasped as though she had been adrift in the Atlantic for a fortnight and Gretel were a sea plane. "You've got to *do* something."

Her voice began a precarious climb skyward.

"That Fred, he's driving me *crazy*. He keeps *look*ing at me and I don't like him. He really *bugs* me. *I mean it!* He *bugs* me. He's trying to make me jealous and I don't even like him."

"Should I tell him you don't like him?" Gretel inquired —calmly, by comparison.

"I don't care *what* you tell him. He really bugs me."

Considerably more conversation ensued, and bits and pieces of the Freddy matter also floated to the surface during lunch hours and other encounters in the hall. What the whole thing added up to was this:

Billy knew that Fred liked her because he had asked another girl for a date. He didn't *like* the other girl; he was taking her out only to make Billy jealous. Billy's saying she didn't like him meant she did like him, and she trusted Gretel to interpret this properly, mention Billy's name to Fred, and report back what he said. The possibility that Fred was taking the other girl to a show because he liked her was dismissed as too horrible to contemplate. For as many weeks as the game could be played, Billy would continue to tell Gretel how much she didn't like Fred so that Gretel would remember to tell her every detail of Fred's physiognomy and posture when the name Billy was mentioned.

Get it?

Avis joined us now and then when she had an armload of Beatle magazines to drop off in Gretel's locker. (She never made her connections outside of lunch hour.) "It's funny after the summer," she said once, as we sprinted along. "Everybody you knew last year you never see to talk to. You just say hi and they run to classes. It's awful. But everybody looks better than last year."

"I don't think so," voiced Cooky from the perimeter. "Some people look worse."

And one day I got a smidgeon of information I found terribly sad. Gretel had returned the stockings she had purchased with such delight on our shopping trip. I suddenly remembered the stockings when I saw her because they would have gone so well with the skirt and sweater she was wearing. I asked her when she was going to wear them and she said never—because her mother didn't like them "and neither did I after a while."

I think about those stockings often. I try to understand why Gretel's mother couldn't let her waste the dollar and a half—if that's what she felt she had done. That single pair of hose had seemed such an important exercise of her taste. She had been allowed to buy herself one special thing on our special afternoon, and then she couldn't keep it. What a sizable shrug she needed to dismiss that little incident.

Gretel. Always promoting me to her friends. Always bolstering me. "Doesn't Lyn look cute today?" she would ask Cooky in the hall. "Hey, did you see Lyn's shoes?" she would demand of Billy. "Aren't they *cute!*"

"Yes, she does," Cooky would have to agree. "Oh, kee-*yooooot*. Let's see. Oh, KEE-OOOOT!" Billy would screech.

Then Gretel would smile and poke me, and I'd look down at the floor. "Aren't they a riot?" she would ask. And I'd nod.

The sounds in the hall. I guess I'll never get them out of my inner ear. Like the exchange between two boys behind me:

"There's that fuck, Alan."

"Who's the shit with him?"

"That's the fuckin guy who lives across the street from him."

"Oh, Christ, that shit."

"Yeah. . . . Hey, Alan, buddy, how'd you do in trig?"

Our first major assignment in English was described to us at the start of the second week of school. It was to be a book report on a work of fiction of the student's own selection. A first draft of the report, in three to five hundred words, was due three weeks from the date of assignment. "Preferably not written in a clothes closet with the lights off," commented Mr. Fells.

"Will you qualify your author, please?" he said. "Tell what else he has written, what honors he has won?"

Mr. Fells also wanted a paragraph on the style of the author. It could be either positive or negative. The main part of the report, however, was to be a subjective reaction to the book.

"We are concentrating on theme," said the teacher. "What was the major idea, the frame of reference? What is he telling you?"

The final draft, he said, we would write in class, after he had had a chance to read our first drafts. We were to spend two days thinking about the books we'd like to read, and then we were to write our choices on a piece of paper which he would pass around.

The piece of paper reached me after seventeen students had indicated their choices on it. There were but six titles on the paper, each selected by two or more students. They were: *My Antonia, The Grapes of Wrath, Lord of the Flies, Uncle Tom's Cabin, The Bad Seed,* and *The Child Buyer.* I wrote *Lord of the Flies* after my own name, and passed the paper to the girl behind me.

Gretel, who sat two rows across from me, told me later that she had also chosen *Lord of the Flies.* I said, "Oh, great, we can write our reports together," which was the proper thing to say, and she said, "*Eeeeeeh,* I know. Isn't that too tough?"

I tried to get a line on what Gretel, and therefore the kids around her to whom she passed notes all through class, thought of Mr. Fells. The most I drew from her, however, was "He's very morbid." Gretel never talked about classes or teachers. She was a poor student, and simply would not concern herself scholastically beyond wishing to get high school over and done with. When homework stumped or overwhelmed her, she just didn't do it. The few times I saw her in the early morning she was usually running around looking for somebody's papers to borrow, or leaning on a locker copying from already borrowed papers. She considered me an intellectual and college material, but did not let this interfere with our relationship.

Little did she dream. . . .

I couldn't even understand instructions. I didn't know, for instance, that when Mr. Fells told us to read "The Pit and the Pendulum" in class and comment on it the next day, he wanted a written report. So when he had the class turn in its homework—"Pass your reports forward, putting your own on top"—there I was, the dunce again. One of three. Had to raise my hand and show everybody. Got a zero for the day. Try living with that at my age.

"The Pit and the Pendulum" was the subject which prompted two boys to raise their hands. While Mr. Fells was still talking, too. The teacher tried to ignore them, but they were waving their arms, stirring the air, so he stopped and nodded toward the one closest to him.

"I saw that movie," said the lad, "and I thought it was very bloody."

Mr. Fells nodded slightly and looked toward the other boy.

But the first boy wasn't finished. "I think Poe was crazy," he said.

"You are entitled to your opinion," said Mr. Fells. "But he was not crazy. He had a very creative mind; he was not writing out of his experience, but out of his imagination."

"You gotta be crazy to imagine those things," said the boy.

"What did you want to say?" asked Mr. Fells of the second boy, cutting the first off at the pass.

"I heard he took dope."

"Who took dope?" asked Mr. Fells, removing his glasses.

"Poe," said the boy.

"We will discuss that later," said Mr. Fells. "Meanwhile, why don't you two sit in these seats here where you can think better?"

Several kids snickered.

"Anybody else want to move?" snapped Mr. Fells.

Quiet.

No more was said about Poe's alleged aberrations. No more was said about anything by the class.

"Now, as I was saying," continued Mr. Fells, replacing his glasses, "Poe had a reason for everything he wrote . . ."

# 20

I'M NOT SURE what Cooky thought would happen when I "got a load" of Georgia's friends, but I certainly was impressed with their underwear. I was so impressed, in fact, that I forgot how nervous I had been about finally facing a real gym class.

I had made quite a point, when I was shopping for my disguises, of buying the proper underwear. And smugly so. How clever of me to remember to dress like a teenager from the skin out, I had thought. A lesser spy would overlook such items and be caught cold in her pretty, mature, ladylike lingerie. Recalling clearly the sort of puritanical unmentionables I had worn in high school, I spent a full hour in the five-and-ten hunting for white cotton bras, briefs, and opaque white half-slips.

Wrong again.

The giggling golden girls disrobing comfortably before a row of lockers adjacent to the gymnasium wore the sexiest nylon underwear I've seen since Sophia Loren stripped in *Yesterday, Today, and Tomorrow*. Black or ecru lace-trimmed bikini pants, matching half-slips with slits up the sides, and matching French-style bras. Not even cute flowered whatsises from the junior department of Gimbels. Not cute anything from anybody's junior department. Naughty, that's what they were. Overtly sex-and-the single-girl things. I was embarrassed to be in the same room with them.

Anyway, I looked like such a square! Holy Hannah, forget the flabby upper arms. Lady, what are you doing in your grandmother's snuggies?

The locker room looked the way it should have. It was a large room lined with gray lockers and wooden benches. There was a half-mirror with a ledge under it across one small wall, and beyond that, a small shower room with sinks, open shower stalls, and closed johns. One door in the locker room led to the gym, another to the playing fields outside. It was through the latter door we were to head within five minutes after the period began.

The first few days I took on this unbelievable procedure, I was completely uncoordinated. I was late to class because I had a mental block, late getting my locker open because I couldn't figure the combination, late getting into my gym suit because I was trying to get undressed behind the open locker door, and late cantering out to the field because I had been late at every other juncture. And let me tell you, it wasn't easy to be the latest one of all in that group of girls who didn't want to play outside . . . but I managed.

Actually, the undressing part wasn't as bad as I had anticipated, thanks to the English alphabet. My name placed me a fairly good distance from the cluster of swingers, and by the time I got down to my skivvies most of the class was gone.

Usually, by the time I got outside, the group was sitting, most in a Buddha posture, at the feet of the teacher. Our teacher was not the main teacher; she was a junior officer. The main teacher came by now and then to inspect.

All the gym teachers, none of whom could be distinguished from any other one, wore short white gym suits with pleated skirts, matching shorts, and white nylon cardigans. They carried clipboards with class rolls on them, and frequently made marks next to names thereon.

Heaven only knows what marks went next to my own. The first day I was so late getting outside that the roll had already been taken and the volley ball and soccer teams already named. After the exercises (what can I tell you —I did push-ups and jumped up and down, and all this right after lunch hour), there was nothing for me to do but stand on the sidelines with two girls who had notes from their doctors saying they couldn't play volley ball when they had cramps. The golden girls were playing soccer, their long blond hair billowing from behind their ears, so I didn't see much of them. One of them asked me to hold her watch while she played, which I gathered was a privilege of sorts. I counted only five golden girls, but there may have been more.

I learned a little about that golden hair, by the way. It was mostly homemade (I never met an Urbanite who went to a hairdresser except for proms), and so worked-over it's a miracle all that glittered weren't also bald. I heard one of Georgia's gang mention that she had tried five different commercial products with names like Moonglow and Sunrise, all within one month. When those had not produced the color she wanted, she rinsed with a succession of kitchen compounds such as tea, lemon juice, and vinegar. Most of the girls had tried setting their hair with beer and were split about fifty-fifty on its benefits.

It was during that first inactive active gym class that I got my only in-depth appraisal of Georgia's gang. It came from one of the girls with cramps, who sat by a pillar with me and talked whenever she thought it was safe. Her name was Trudy.

She began our conversation with "You're new, aren't

you? Where're you from?" She mentioned she'd seen "Jill" hand me her watch, and went on from there. This I gathered from her chatter, some of which I provoked with comments of my own:

Georgia and her gang had rich parents and boyfriends with sports cars. They set the fashion among juniors at Urban, they controlled the class elections, they gave the only good parties, and they were a closed society. They inter-dated, and they didn't want any new members. Most of them had grown up together. Most talked about going to college, though some had gone steady so long they'd probably get married right after graduation and "have babies right away."

Trudy was impressed by the gang and intimidated by it. "They can do anything they want and get away with it," she said with a sigh and a shrug. What she envied most was their cool. "They just never lose their cool" was the way she put it. "You know they care about everything, but they just never show it."

Later on, Trudy became a real problem for me. She brought a friend over to meet me, a girl who had also lived recently in New York, the one who had recognized me by my Pappagallos. This girl knew a lot of the kids from my high school, she said. And thus began another one of those incredible scenes I seemed to find myself in every other turn of the moon—with this kid from New York tailing me all over the soccer field dropping names of kids she thought I should know. I couldn't shake her. If I said I'd never been to any of Alan Krantz's parties, she asked me if I knew Richy Shuman. When I didn't know Richy, even though she couldn't imagine that, since he was head cheerleader at my old high school, she wondered then if I ever saw Sybil Berken or any of those kids. After about the third time I missed kicking the ball because of her spooking around, I couldn't help wondering if she was trying to trick me. Suppose they were made-up names, and I said I knew one and she said, "just as I thought, you are not really from South Suburban."

I ducked and I bobbed and I weaved, impressing all with my vigor on the soccer field. In fact, I got a pat on the back from one of the gym teachers. "Nice try," she said. "Keep it up." Still, I could not get rid of what's-her-name from New York. I finally turned my back on her and said, "I didn't know anybody at South Suburban; I was sick," and she shrugged and left me alone. But any time I looked her way in gym class, I caught her staring at me.

I had another scare in gym. One that nearly shattered me for good. I rushed in late one afternoon, so late the locker room was nearly empty, got as far as my locker, and heard my name being called loudly and angrily by one of the gym teachers.

"Are you Tornabene?" she shouted.

I nodded.

"Come over here, young lady. We've been waiting for you."

I did as I was told.

"You're in real trouble, young lady," she said, looking first at me and then at her clipboard. "Come with me."

She led me to the small office where the head gym teacher sat behind a desk.

"This is Tornabene," she said.

The head gym teacher fingered a pencil on her desk, then looked up at me, sternly, for a full minute.

"How old are you, young lady?" she demanded.

"Sixteen and a half," I whispered.

"Sixteen and a half?" she repeated.

I nodded.

"Well, then, you're old enough to know how to take care of a locker, aren't you?"

I didn't understand her.

"Do you know what you did yesterday?" she barked.

I shook my head no.

"You left your locker combination on the sink. You didn't know that, did you?"

I shook my head again and suddenly realized I was going to cry.

"Well, it's just lucky I found the paper and not some thief."

I nodded and swallowed.

She went on about lockers and thieves and responsibilities, but I didn't hear her clearly until she said, "You can go now. But if you ever do this again, I'll flunk you. Do you understand?"

I nodded.

The junior officer was touched by my condition. She patted my arm.

"I . . . I'm new here and I have so much to remember, I guess I just can't," I said.

"That's all right. You'll catch on," she assured me. "Take your time getting dressed and then you can play volley ball in place of Alberts today."

"Thank you," I said.

Only one of Georgia's gang ever spoke to me in gym class. I don't know what her name was, though it could well have been Jill because she looked like Jill. She shouted at me from the bench in front of her locker, where she sat in her black bikini underwear, her bikini tan still even from summer sunning.

"Hey," she said, "you know David Bodine, don't you?"

"Uh-hunh," I said.

"How'd you get to meet *him* so fast? You're new here, aren't you?"

"Uh-hunh," I said.

"How'd you get to know him, then?"

"His mother knows my mother."

"Are you going with him?"

"Oh no," I said in as high a pitch as I could muster. "We're just friends."

"I'll bet," she said, stepping into her skirt. (She didn't even *wear* a half-slip.)

Very cool, that girl. But I was, too, don't you think?

I was even cooler after I took the required showers. Took them just like in the good old days: first hot, then cold, amidst shrieks of "It's too *hot!*" and "*eeeeeeh,* it's too *cold!*" Took them practically wrapped in a towel, just like in the good old days. Looked neither to the left nor to the right. Ran like hell, into the shower, out of the shower. Managed, by heaven, to get through the whole thing without getting my eyeglasses wet.

Following which, I ran up to the first floor, around to the other side of the building, up to the second floor—two steps at a time when the way was clear—across the bridge to the annex, and up another flight of steps to speech class, where Mr. Roth waited at the door watching his watch.

There was always an air of tension in that room, rising off the taut forms of the students. All of them sat at the ready, leaving their heads loose to be able to follow Mr. Roth as he paced the aisles or sat down in the back of the room, or leaned against his podium. One never knew where he would turn up, taunting, and teasing, and playing games with his voice.

"This is what I mean by voice projection. Not this: THIS DOESN'T MEAN YOU ARE PROJECTING, IT ONLY MEANS YOU ARE SHOUTING. This means you are projecting. You see how you can hear me clearly from here . . . or here . . . or here.

215

"Now you do it. *You.* That's right, I don't mean her. I mean you. Unless you are a her. Are you a her? No? Well, good, I didn't think so."

Each day he gave a new assignment which could be started in class and finished at home, but which had to be fully prepared by the next day. None was ever mentioned again. I continued to do my speech homework every night because I was afraid Mr. Roth would one day demand it all, but I doubt that the rest of the class bothered. There were no living people in that room anyway. Just bodies conditioned to duck when necessary. This is a typical scene from speech class:

Mr. Roth, for the day's assignment, instructed each member of the class to interview some other member of the class and prepare an introduction of that person for everyone else in the room.

"Now pair off and get to work," he ordered when he had finished describing what he wanted.

Nobody moved.

"Get partners," he said. "Each of you, get someone to work with."

Nobody moved.

"Do I have to hold your hands? Get partners."

Nothing. Except I moved. I poked the girl in front of me and suggested we work together. She shrugged and turned toward me.

"How old are you?" she asked. That wasn't essential to the assignment, but that's all she wanted to know.

"Sixteen and a half," I said. "What's your name? Where are you from?"

She answered my two questions in three words: "Carolyn Phelp. Here." And she turned back to her desk.

The long-haired boy with the paint on his clothes paired off with another fey young man, but no one else

216

did a thing. Mr. Roth sat at his desk, pretending to read, pretending we were doing our homework.

Indeed, I could see why any teacher might go mad having to deal daily with such lethargy, but I had no sympathy for Mr. Roth. I found his performances shocking, his methods sadistic. He brought out the very worst in me. So threatened did I feel by his authority that I let my guard drop time after time in his classroom. For instance:

One afternoon he was preparing the class for a demonstration of the use of dramatics in public speaking. In order to do so, he rearranged our seating so we made a better-distributed audience; he made sure there were people in all the key spots around the room. ("Can you make it all right?" he asked one boy who was on his way to the back of the room. "I wouldn't want you to break a leg or anything.") Then he gave a vocal demonstration, and went on to talk about celebrities who made use of dramatics in public speaking.

"Adlai Stevenson was one of the great actors of our time," he said. "So was John F. Kennedy. Does anyone know any others?"

Silence.

"None?"

Silence.

"None at all? You people aren't very bright, are you?"

Silence.

Then a deep, nasal voice, with broad projection and an Eastern accent, declared, "Franklin Roosevelt."

Everyone looked around to locate the source of the voice. I, who knew from whom it had come, could only blush.

"Hey, what grade are you in?" demanded the girl newly seated in front of me.

217

"Sixteen and a half," I mumbled.

"Huh?" she said.

And the bell rang ending the period.

There were other, similar incidents, too small or too oblique to describe. And then, one Friday, Mr. Roth was trying to show his students how badly they talked by mimicking them, one by one, after he called on them and got them to speak. He had left two boys and a girl in crumpled heaps of embarrassment by the time he turned to me and asked, "What do you suppose makes you speak the way you do?"

I didn't want to fall into his trap, and indeed I didn't have to. All I had to do was act like a teenager: shrug and remain silent. But I didn't. Instinctively, I became myself. I leaned back in my chair, looked up at him, and clearly and confidently asked, "What do you mean? How do I speak?"

And a very strange thing happened. Mr. Roth looked stunned. Every pair of eyes in the class riveted on the two of us. He looked at me quickly, said, "We'll discuss it later," and walked away, visibly disturbed.

Just as quickly as I had responded, I realized the critical mistake I had made. Students simply did not challenge teachers in the classes I attended. It was obvious, frequently, that a student didn't understand a question he was asked, but he would never say so. He would shrug, mumble, shrink, fail—anything but imply that the teacher had not communicated. The other alternative, to risk giving the wrong answer, was too terrible even to imagine. A wrong answer usually prompted derisive snickers around the room, and the worst punishment of all was scorn from one's peers.

Drawing a line on what is to be endured, I discovered at Urban, is a privilege of age. That's why I made a wave

218

when I asked Mr. Roth to elaborate on his question. As far as he and the class knew, I was not old enough to dare. And by daring, I had brought an intensity of attention to myself which I could not afford.

That, I believe, was the moment I decided I had to go home. I told myself I'd see what happened on the weekend and then make up my mind, but my mind was already made up. My days at Urban were having such a strange effect on me, my own mind was growing to be so unfamiliar, that I was feeling physically ill.

I simply could not bend enough. I could not give up enough of my personality. I was afraid that if I did let myself succumb enough to go on passing—succumb was what I felt I had to do—there would be nothing left of me as an adult. My lack of school records had to be discovered before many more weeks passed. The traits that seemed odd about me to my teenage friends would seem odder and odder. It was inevitable that I would be caught, one way or another. And if, in the interim, I stayed around acting juvenile more and more successfully, I felt, by the time the inevitable happened, I would be a real teenager. It was as though I were being gone over every day by a steam iron held tightly by someone determined to press out all of my wrinkles.

I barely thought of Frank, or my family, or my friends. My husband's letters describing what was going on at home were as meaningful to me as wire-service reports from New Zealand. I wasn't reading newspapers, magazines, or books. I didn't know or care if the bomb had been dropped. I didn't think about anything but girl friends, teachers, classes, and, well, boys—or my lack of appeal to them. I was worrying about whether or not I was homely, and I was spending more hours than I care to enumerate staring in mirrors. I was looking forward to David's party as though it were a real social occasion in

my life instead of a great opportunity to observe. I was
having frightening dreams about being late to class, not
finishing homework, being scolded, being lost. And I
hated Mr. Roth.

It was time to go home.

# 21

THOUGH GRETEL had often asked me to "do something" on Saturdays, I'd never been able to spare the time away from my notebook and personal chores. Now I was determined to make the time, and so I called her about ten in the morning. That phone call went like this:

"Hi, Gretel? It's me."

"Oh, *hi*. You're up early."

"So are you."

Giggle. "That's true. I'm not really awake yet though."

"Me either."

Giggle.

"Listen, are you doing anything today?" (That's my voice.)

"Hold on a second, will you? (*Aside:* What time are you leaving? What time are you coming back? Before lunch? Oh, after lunch. How late? Okay.) I had to talk to my mother. She's going out."

"Are you alone?"

"No, but I will be in a minute. *Yeeeeeee!*"

"Yippeeeeee." Laughter.

"Anyway, I was thinking. Would you like to take a bus ride and look around a little?"

"Sure, I'd love to."

"Okay. Good. I'll call Cooky about twelve when she gets up."

Giggle.

"What'll I do, meet you somewhere?"

"Oh gee, that's right. Well, listen, do you think you could come here? I don't know where you live. But you don't know where I live either, do you?"

"That's okay. Maybe my guardian can bring me over."

"Oh, great. I'll tell you how to get here."

"Wait a minute. I'll get something to write with." (I copied down Gretel's directions.)

"What time will you come?"

"Gee. I'm not sure. Not before twelve, I guess. Is that too late?"

"Unh-unh. That's fine."

"I didn't eat breakfast yet."

"Me either." Giggle.

"And I have a couple of things to do."

"Me too. I've got to . . . let's see . . . get dressed."

"Yes, do that."

Another giggle. "And clean up my room . . . and feed George—"

"Who's George?"

"My puppy, silly. You didn't meet my puppy yet, did you? Wait, I'll put him on the phone. . . . C'mere, George. C'mon. Say hello to Lyn. Say hello. . . . He doesn't want to talk now. You can see him later. He's so *cute.*"

"What color is he?"

"Brown. Light brown. With a little white on his paws."

"Ohhhhhh. That's cute. I love puppies."

"I took him to the pet show last night and introduced him to the monkeys. He loved them."

"Ahhhhhh."

"You'll see him. He's so dear."

"Listen, what'll we wear?"

"Slacks?"

"Yes, I'd love to. But I don't have slacks, exactly, they're jeans."

"That's what I have, too, jeans."

"Swell, then. We'll wear jeans. Maybe I could bring a skirt along in case, well, if it's not right. I could bring it in my pocketbook or something."

"If you want to."

"Oh, well, I won't if I don't have to."

"You don't have to. All the kids wear—"

"Good, then. I'll just wear jeans and a shirt. Okay? A shirt?"

"Yes, fine."

"And . . . sneakers, I think. Sneakers?"

"Sure."

"Swell. That's perfect. How much money do you have?"

"Gee, about a dollar-seventy, I think. How much do you have?"

"I don't know. About two dollars. Maybe I can borrow some more from my guardian. Do you think we need more?"

"Maybe." Giggle. "Take anything you can get."

"Okay. I'll see you later, then."

"That's great. You sure you know how to get here? It's the house right across from a big brick thing that looks like a church."

"Okay. I'll find it."

"Okeydoke. Wait a minute. George wants to say goodbye. . . . No, he doesn't. Oh, well. Bye."

When Bess dropped me off, precisely at one, Gretel was at an upstairs window of her house, a pretty place in a good neighborhood. Bess sped away so she wouldn't be

223

seen, but she was too late. Gretel greeted me with "Was that your guardian? I love her station wagon. And she's pretty. I thought she'd be older."

"She is older," I said. "She just looks young."

The house was well furnished with contemporary furniture, but there was something oddly cold about the interior. Everything looked as though it had been purchased within the past two years. There were no memories in it, no foolishness. Only Gretel's room had a past, and thereby a warmth, and we lingered there while she showed me her souvenirs. It was a large room, monastically bare. It had only her bed in it, a small dresser, and a chair. There were lots of stuffed animals around, though, and a bulletin board covered with pictures cut from magazines, cartoons, photographs, and assorted mementos. She showed me dozens of photographs of boyfriends she had left behind as she was handed from relative to relative around the country. She showed me pictures of her boyfriends' cars, a picture of herself with her ex at last year's prom, and finally, a picture of the cabin her stepfather was building on a nearby lake.

"You'll have a wonderful time there," I said.

"Oh, it only has room for two to sleep comfortably," she said lightheartedly. "They'll be going there a lot of weekends when it's finished. But I don't mind. I'll have somebody come and stay with me. Maybe you will. Will you? It'll be fun. Cooky stays alone all the time and she says it's fun. Now that I'm not going steady anymore, I won't have to have any adults around. If I was still going steady they'd *never* let me stay here alone. They'd think . . . you know . . ."

Gretel wanted to play some records, so we went into the dining room where there was a console phonograph. "We could use my old machine but this one is so much better," she said. "Whenever there's nobody home, I play

224

it. Listen." She put on some rock-'n'-roll albums and we sat on the floor. George, a chubby, three-month-old cocker spaniel, joined us, and Gretel told me all about his care and feeding. She loved him very much. And he her.

She asked me if I had had a steady in New York and, when I said yes, asked to see a picture of him. I was carrying a small photo of Frank in my wallet, taken when he was in his twenties, I believe. It was a long-distance shot of him in a woods with shadows all over him, and I had figured it was safe to carry. In fact, he was so obscure, the photo could well have been taken from a helicopter hovering at twelve hundred feet.

"He looks old," said Gretel.

"Um," I said. "He's in college."

"But he's cute," she said.

I nodded.

"Are you going to marry him?" she inquired.

I said I didn't know if I'd ever even see him again.

"Oh dear, that's right," she said. "Well, maybe he'll come out here someday."

"Maybe," I said.

She turned up the sound on the phonograph so I could hear every lyric that was rocking-'n'-rolling out of it.

"Isn't that great?" she said, rocking.

I nodded enthusiastically.

We talked about her ex, Arnie, and the fact that he was dating Roxanne now. I had told her this after the football game, and she had had immediate hysterics. She recovered from them in time to prevent me from killing myself for being so callous, but I was never sure I should have been the one to bring her the news. Everything about the Seth football game had horrified her, and she had shrieked and laughed and scolded me when I reported on it. "You're starting off all wrong," she had said. "What if your guardian found out?" Then she had thought

225

it over and decided I couldn't have done anything but what I did. "Oh, well," she had said, "if everybody went you *had* to go."

She told me that Arnie was really very nasty. She had said so before, but I still didn't get it, so I asked her in what way.

"Well, he tries things," she said. "You can tell him no and put him off, but he tries. Roxanne was hanging around him a lot, you know. She thinks I hate her now, but I don't. She used to go with . . . did you see the cute cheerleader with the blond hair? Well, him. They broke up last summer."

She sighed.

"Listen," she said, perking up. "Let's go out and get something to eat and look around. I'll call Cooky."

"I don't think Cooky likes me," I said.

"Sure she does," Gretel said. "That's the way she is. You'll get used to her. She's really great."

Cooky's line was busy. "That girl can really gab on the phone," Gretel reported. "She doesn't even get up till noon and then she goes right to the phone." When Gretel finally reached her, she stayed on the phone for thirty minutes talking mostly about Roxanne, love, and life. I wandered around the house and came back to hear her winding up:

"That's the way it was with me, too. I would have been engaged. By the end of this year I would have had a ring, and next year I would have been married."

Whatever that was about, it gave me chills. Gretel, married in a year. God. But happening every day if we can believe the oft-quoted statistic that 13 per cent of American brides marry before they are eighteen.

She made me say hi to Cooky and then took back the phone to find out if her friend wanted to go to "a show" with her that night. Cooky evidently asked what was playing, because Gretel went for the paper and read the ads to her, with comments like "That got good reviews" or "Ugh." The conversation ended with Gretel's promise to call Cooky the minute she got home from wherever she and I were going.

"You know what Cooky said?" Gretel began as we walked up a street near her house. "Nobody ever said this to me before. I think it's very smart. She said that I don't really like Arnie anymore at all, I just miss him because we used to go everywhere together. She said that if I met some real cute guy I wouldn't even think about Arnie anymore. I never thought about it like that. I think she's right, really."

We walked as far as a bus stop and then took a long bus ride through sections of the town I had never seen. We got out at one point and bought a couple of slices of pizza which I ate ravenously and Gretel just nibbled. "My stepfather says my eyes are bigger than my stomach," she said. (My father used to say that about me, too, but never regarding pizza; when I was Gretel's age there was no such thing as pizza in small U.S. towns. Fancy growing up without pizza. Unthinkable.)

Later we got ice cream cones—or, at least, I got an ice cream cone—and sat on a bench and talked. (Today's teenagers don't eat like yesterday's, you know. I hadn't known that. I'd thought that the one really great thing about this trip would be the food. I'd thought I would finally and legitimately have a milk shake after all these years, and a hot fudge sundae and a hamburger with French fries and lemon cream pie, too. I'd figured, of course, that I would weigh three hundred pounds by the time I came home, but I was all wrong. I was eating nothing and I was shedding weight like the incredible shrinking man.)

Anyway.

I told Gretel I thought Billy swore a lot, and she concurred, doing a great imitation of some of Billy's best invectives. I said Billy swore a lot in front of the bearded guy and his friend, and Gretel said she shouldn't do that because guys don't like it. Guys only like Billy as a friend, she told me.

I told her about the fifteen-year-old girl Bess had told me about, the one who picked up the soldier, and so on. She was shocked. She said, "She *did?* Boy, why'd she do that? She's crazy." Then admiration got the best of her and she asked, "How'd she do it? What does she look like?"

I told her I didn't know.

She said, "You know that guy who sits next to me in English class? I like him. At Nina's party last year? I kissed him. I mean he kissed me. And I danced with him a lot. Arnie got really mad. He said, 'Come on, let's go.' He never dated anyone else. I did, when he was sick. But I told him. I never dated anyone without telling him. And I could have. When you go steady, you lose a lot of friends because they always see you with him and they figure why bother to ask you to go shopping or anything because you're always with *him.*"

She told me she would like to have a *big* party but couldn't because her house was too close to the other houses and everybody would complain. Parties are usually crashed, she said.

"You send out these little invitations to the people you want and then everybody hears about it and comes too. At Maureen's party her sister was really mean. She wouldn't let anybody in. She stood at the door and said, 'You don't have an invitation, you can't come in.' She made some guys leave because they brought bottles."

I told her the guys at home drank a lot of beer. She said, "Out here they drink everything."

"Where do they get it?" I asked.

She answered, "Angela has a fake I.D. card. And some stores don't even ask for identification. They sell anybody who has the money."

I asked her if she had had a sixteenth-birthday party.

"No," she said, "that's childish. I told somebody I wanted to have one and she said, 'oh, grow up.' I like parties with a theme. Roxanne had one in her garage. It was Hawaiian and it was so completely *tough*. We wore muumuus and she decorated the garage and it was really tough."

"What did she have to eat?" I asked.

"Oh, it was really cool: dips and little sandwiches and everything to drink."

Later we went to a discount store and looked at every single item on the shelves. Gretel was as interested in pots and pans and gourmet food as I was. We fingered everything. Then we stopped in front of the cosmetics counter and just stood, like a pair of confused robots. I picked up a lipstick to buy, but Gretel shook her head no.

"I like to deal in name brands," she said.

I replaced the lipstick.

Gretel found a belt she *loved*—it was "so tough, so cute, so great, so cheap." Only seventy-nine cents. She tried it on, walked around, laid it down, picked it up, strolled away from it, dashed back to it. She decided to buy it and she was elated.

"Wait till everyone *sees* it," she said with pure joy; pure, unadulterated joy. "Oh, you get one, too, Lyn. Please." She skipped around and looked for another, found one, and ran it back to me. She made me try it on and said it looked great, darling, so cute. We would wear them together and just wait till everyone saw them, they'd die. And we wouldn't tell anyone where we got them. She asked me to promise I would wear it on Monday because she would wear hers on Monday. I promised.

Do you remember? A belt or a wallet or a kerchief or

socks or an I.D. bracelet, one for you and one for your friend?

Promise. What a word.

We had a wonderful day. *I* had a wonderful day. I was sorry when it was over.

It ended with an elaborate lie. Gretel asked me to go to the show with her and Cooky, and instead of saying I had to go to a party, I told her that I'd gotten a strange telegram. My father was flying in to see me, I said, and my guardian was taking me to the airport to pick him up.

"Gee, do you think he'll take you home?" she asked.

"I don't know what he wants," I said. "I don't even know what I'll say to him."

She assured me all would be well. "Just say to him 'Hi, Dad!' and be real sweet and everything. Tell him everything's fine. It'll be fun."

I nodded.

"Call me in the morning and tell me everthing that happens," she said, leaving me at a bus stop. And as the bus pulled up, she hollered over the noise of its motor in that silly voice with the crooked pitch, "Don't forget about the belts. The *belts*."

# 22

**M**Y DATE telephoned several times while I was out with Gretel. Bess said he had sounded disturbed and asked that I call him, please, as soon as I got back.

"Maybe the party's off," she suggested. I gave her a dirty look for giving the gods the idea, and also for making me nervous.

The party wasn't off. When I phoned David, he said he had wanted me to go with him to a meeting of the Young Democrats Club. He thought I should attend that sort of meeting so I could see another facet of teenage life, and he was disappointed not to find me available. But it turned out to be okay, anyway, he said, because the YDC president didn't show up and the meeting was canceled.

"You still want to go tonight?" David asked.

I said I did. He said, "Well, it'll probably be a big bore."

He wanted to know if I could get the car again, and I told him I could. He found that "a relief."

I was to pick him up at nine, and Bess should give me the directions to his house.

"Okay?"

Okay.

And listen, he said, it would be better if I didn't wear my glasses. It would be very dark at the party and I really wouldn't need them.

"Okay?"

Okay.

I wore an olive-green, ridiculously short, wraparound wool skirt; an orange-colored, lightweight wool turtleneck sweater which Bess loaned me ("Looks very good— covers the lines on your neck, ha-ha"); stockings; Pappagallos; and no eyeglasses. I carried my fuzzy sweater.

David wore a pair of cotton slacks that looked like gray chinos, a white shirt, and a periwinkle-blue Perry Como sweater which he preferred to call an Andy Williams cardigan. As my mother used to say when I was in high school, that's not the way people used to dress for parties.

In the car I asked him who would be at the party, and he shrugged. "Nancy won't," he said.

"Who's Nancy?"

"The girl I like."

"I didn't know you liked one particular girl."

"Yeah," he said.

"Does she like you?" I asked.

He shrugged. "I'm working on it."

I wished him luck, and then felt strangely uncomfortable. "Did you want to take her to the party tonight?" I asked.

"She had to baby-sit," he replied.

"Oh," I said.

Silence.

"Well, does she know you're taking me to the party?"

"Yeah, I told her."

"What did she say?"

"She asked me if I like you."

"And what did you say?"

"I told her you were old enough to be my mother."

232

"That's great," I said, sounding as disturbed as I felt.

"Why, what's the matter with that?" David wanted to know.

"You told her what I'm doing here?" I asked.

"She won't tell anybody. She can keep a secret better than you can."

I suggested that he was a real buddy, and he looked hurt.

"I had to tell her," he said.

We ended the subject right there.

In a few minutes I met Nancy. And let me tell you, that was pretty weird.

We drove to the house where the party was being held, but David didn't want to go in because there were no cars out front. I said, "Let's go get a Coke," and he said, "Let's go see Nancy." I said I didn't want to see Nancy and he said, "I told her we would."

"You did what?" I asked.

He smiled. "She's waiting for us. I told her we'd be there right after nine."

Nancy was cute as a Lolita-bunny. Tiny and stacked, she appeared terribly young, maybe fourteen, but also terribly old. She had big, dark, slanted eyes, lightly made up, and dark brown hair that she wore like Angela's, pinned up and wispy. She had on black stretch pants and a modest white overblouse. She had a bright, lively look about her.

She made me feel like somebody's mother-in-law.

"Hi," she said.

"Hi," I said. And we tried not to stare at each other.

The six-year-old boy she was sitting with was still up, so that helped. We all talked about him. Eventually, though, she and David got engrossed in each other in a bear-cub kind of way, and I looked around for a pit to drop into.

They giggled and poked each other and hit each other

and giggled some more. And I remembered, as vividly as though it had been last month, having the same kind of playfully physical meetings with the love of my teenage life. I remembered never being able to keep my hands off him. I'd slap him, push him, pull on his sweater—any excuse to touch him. The kids at Urban did a lot of that kind of puppying around, too, during lunch hour.

But I don't know, I was embarrassed with David and Nancy. Clearly they wanted to be alone, and clearly some of their giggling was brought on by the presence of me in my costume, and, worse yet, nothing was said about my reason for being in costume in the first place.

Fortunately, we didn't stay long. When David indicated we were about to leave, I went out to the car to allow him time to say goodbye. He was grinning when he joined me.

"She thinks you're very nice," he said.

"I think she is, too," I volunteered. "And cute. Really cute."

"Yeah, she is, isn't she?" said David. Then he laughed.

I did, of course, ask him why.

"I think she's jealous," he said.

"Of me?"

"Uh-hunh. I think you just did me a lot of good."

"I'm glad," I said. "I owed you a favor."

As we walked up the driveway toward the location of the big event, three attractive boys were walking toward us. Two said "Hi" and walked on. The other stopped and signaled thumbs down. "Check out," he advised. "No booze." Then he moved on.

"I told you so," said David.

"For God's sake, come on already," I suggested sweetly.

Inside it was so dark I couldn't tell whether the person who greeted us at the door was male or female until it

234

shrieked "Hi, David." It was female. "Everybody's outside," she said.

The outside, consisting of a small patio and yard, was prettily lighted with Chinese lanterns and candles in hurricane lamps. In the glow I could see several clusters of girls of what I have come to call the pierced-ears variety. They were fifteen to sixteen-and-a-half years old, privileged, bright, but not go-go. All together, there must have been fifteen or so of them, and most were dressed in slacks or dark Bermudas, with shirts or sweaters or T-shirts. They were standing in an assortment of uncomfortable postures, fidgeting with themselves, waiting. A few in each group kept their eyes fixed on the doorway.

In fewer clusters, usually centering around a single male figure, were about ten boys—two or three, I thought after a quick appraisal, cute-looking in their sweaters and slacks. Rock-'n'-roll music sounded out of a portable phonograph, but nobody was dancing. David, with me two steps behind him and silent, stopped at each cluster to accept an effusive greeting, then took up a position by the phonograph with me and three girls who immediately started to giggle. When the first quake of contact subsided, they talked about school, and who had seen whom, where, since their trip to Europe.

"What happened to Richy Berns?"

"His mother sent him to military school."

"Hey, Norma's going with Alan Axelrod now."

"Oh, no! You're kidding."

"No, honest."

"Since when?"

"Since right before school started."

I sidled over to David and asked which of the kids went to Super with him, and he pointed out three girls and two boys. The rest went to other local high schools and private schools. None went to Urban; we were in the wrong section of town for Urbanites.

At any desperate lull, one group fingered record albums and made comments like "Oh, play this" and "*That* group, they're all queer" and my favorite one: "Tex Beneke (pronounced Ben-eek), who's *that?*"

Several times my date was called to the telephone. When he left, I stood quietly in the shadows, watching and listening. Two couples, who were dating and had come in together, were reminiscing about the summer's most hilarious moments, and they tried to explain them to the rest of us standing at the phonograph. What they were describing had something to do with three days of turmoil over underwear at a resort where all their parents had summer houses. As best as I could figure the succession of events, the boy cousin of one of the girls standing with us had pinned a pair of her panties on a bulletin board. She and her girl friends had retaliated by stealing all the boys' underwear, fastening it together, and running it up the flag pole. Whereupon all the boys stole all the girls' underwear and buried it somewhere where it is still hidden, a treasure some fortunate soul will one day happen upon.

The audience for this story was not nearly as broken up by it as the couples telling it. All the punctuation came from the narrators: "Oh, you did so" and "Well, I couldn't help it" and "He almost died" and "My mother dropped dead when I had to go buy all new pants" and "Well, *he* started it" and "Oh, he *did* not, you big liar" and "You're *terrible*" and "Wait, let Jane tell that part" and "Oh, stop it, it was *not!*"

David returned from each of his phone calls with what Billy would term a chicken-shit grin on his face, and I was getting more and more curious about who was calling him. I figured it was Nancy, but I was wrong. It was three other girls. Three girls who had been planning to come to the party because of David's presence, but had heard that he had a date and were upset.

"What'd you tell them?" I asked.

"I said you weren't my date," he replied.

"Who are they?" I asked.

"Just some girls," he said.

"You know a lot of girls," I suggested.

He smiled.

Four more young men arrived in a group, and that caused another quake. One of them, the leader of the pack, was a local hero, and his coming had been anticipated somewhat like a more famous Biblical one.

"*Turner!*"

"*Turner!*"

"*Turner!*"

"Turner, baby!"

"Hi, everyone," said Turner, a five-foot ten-inch, husky, dark-haired, older fellow. Seventeen. Captain of the basketball team. Already accepted for college. Sports scholarship. Hands in pockets. Humble. Regular. *Unattached.* (Just broke up with Cristy.) BUICK CONVERTIBLE.

David decided Turner was for me. "Come on, I'll fix it," he said.

He went over to talk to Turner, and then all of a sudden (honest, Frank, I had nothing to do with it) I was dancing this sort of fox-trot with the captain of the basketball team. He didn't ask me, exactly, he just walked at me holding out his right arm.

It was very funny. He held me at full arm's length, so lightly and awkwardly I barely knew which direction he was going in from one step to another. We hardly talked. We didn't look at each other. Every now and then I felt somebody should say something, so I'd say "I go to Ur-

237

ban" or "I just got here" or "This is a nice house, isn't it?"
Turner answered in monosyllables or grunts, backing far-
ther away with each sound.

When the dance ended we stood next to each other, not
saying anything. I assumed he was dying to get rid of me,
and looked around for David, humming indifferently. Before I could get away, however, a Beatle album was put on
the machine. Turner's knees buckled, his head lolled, his
arms stiffened, and his eyes closed. He was dancing. He
didn't say anything to me about joining him, but he was
dancing in front of me, so I figured, Oh hell, why not? (I
happen to be very fond of the frug, anyway.) So we
frugged opposite each other, and in time everybody else
on the patio was dancing—lots of the girls alone, because
there weren't enough guys to go around—and it was just
like you see on television.

David wasn't dancing, though. He was standing by the
phonograph, laughing at me. I think he had put on the
Beatle album, but I can't prove it.

Dripping wet beneath my bangs and my turtleneck
sweater, I went wherever Turner went, not as far out, of
course, but in the same direction. When at last the music
ended, Turner straightened, looked around for his
buddies, said, "Well, see ya" to me, and flaked off.

I stood alone in the middle of the patio for a moment,
catching my breath, and then shuffled to David's side, a
failure. What do you suppose I did wrong? David
wouldn't tell me.

"Come on, let's go inside. That's where the action is," he
said.

When my eyes grew accustomed to the dark, I focused
on two couples necking on the couch, and one couple
necking on the floor. None had come to the party together. Those were "pickups," my date informed me.

We hung in the middle of the room, pivoting. In time

238

we were joined by a young man not much taller than I, well-dressed, and eager. David flaked off. The young man hung on. "You're from New York, aren't you?" he asked me. I nodded. He leaped. He was dying to go to New York. Man, that was his kind of city. When he got out of school next summer, he was going to head straight for Manhattan. He had applied to N.Y.U. and Columbia. He wanted to get into the ad game, man, where the real money was.

He talked in longer sentences than I had heard since I left home, and there seemed to be no end to what he had to say. He asked me if he could get me something to eat from the dining room, and ran to do so when I nodded my permission. He returned with cake and ice cream and punch, which I balanced delicately as he talked about his trip to Europe. Meanwhile, the two couples on the couch went quietly upstairs. I caught David's eye as they did so, and he smiled and shrugged.

Steven, which was the name of the fellow attached to my sleeve, asked if I'd like to sit down on the empty couch, but I said I'd rather stand.

We ate silently for a minute, Steven smiling at me whenever I glanced at him. Then, after swallowing, he asked, conversationally, "Have you ever tried marijuana?"

"Gee, no," I said. "Have you?"

"Unh-unh," he said, "but I have a cousin who has. His friend smokes it all the time."

"Gee," I said.

"Well, he's older," said Steven. "He's in college. But it doesn't hurt you, you know."

"It doesn't?" I inquired.

"Unh-unh. Not like smoking cigarettes does. I read that. It's not habit-forming either—I read that, too. It's not nearly as bad for you as drinking."

"No kidding?"

"Unh-unh. I'd like to try it someday."

"Gee, I wouldn't," I said. Steven shrugged. "Where can you get it?" I asked him.

"In Greenwich Village," he said.

"You mean in New York?" I asked.

"Sure," he said.

"Where in Greenwich Village?" I asked.

"Oh, anyplace. You just get out of a bus and ask somebody. Or you ask a cabdriver."

"Gee, that's interesting," I said. "But that's pretty far away. Where do you get it around here?"

"Oh, there are guys who know," Steven assured me.

"Name one," I said.

He poked my arm. "You don't think I'm going to tell *you*, do you?"

"Why can't you tell me?" I asked in my highest pitch.

" 'Cause you're too young," said Steven.

"Oh, I am *not*. You're just being mean," I said. "I bet you don't know where to get it."

"I do so," Steven insisted. "I could get some if I wanted to. There are always guys hanging around."

"Well, I think you're crazy," I said.

"No, you are," he said lovingly.

Then we were quiet again.

"Did you ever go out with a fem?" he asked me with a mouth full of cake.

"What's *that*?" I responded.

"A queer. A faggot. You know, a fairy."

"Unh-unh," I said.

"Two times when I was in France, queers tried to pick me up," he said.

"No kidding?" I commented.

"No. Honest. And once coming home on the boat, one almost raped me."

I gasped in horror and looked at Steven a bit more closely. Could be, I thought.

The party was growing, and indeed there was trouble at the door where our hostess was trying to keep out crashers. The patio was quite filled with dancers and the living room floor was getting filled with loungers. David was sitting on the floor between two girls, but got up from time to time to take phone calls.

"Everybody knows I brought you," he whispered on one of his treks.

"Why is that such big news?" I whispered back, but he disappeared before I could get an answer.

The vacant couch was taken, eventually, by one girl and two boys with guitars. When the other living room dwellers spotted the guitars, they gathered on the floor in front of the couch and stretched out. One of the boys began to tune up. "Come on, Stretch, you, too," everybody hollered, so Stretch tuned up. Both began to play chords, looking very serious.

"Sing, Tony," pleaded a girl on the floor. Other voices urged him on, too. He and Stretch continued to play chords, never taking their eyes off their own hands.

"When I was just a lad of ten, my father said to me," sang Tony in a pleasing young voice, "come here and take a lesson from the lovely lemon tree. Don't put your faith in love, my boy, my father said to me. I fear you'll find that love is like the lovely lemon tree."

Stretch joined him in the chorus, his voice deeper and louder: "Lemon tree very pretty and the lemon flower is sweet, But the fruit of the poor lemon is impossible to eat."

Tony sang the next verse, and when Stretch joined in the chorus, several girls sang along:

"Lemon tree, very pretty, and the lemon flower is sweeeeeeet, but the fruit of the lemon is impossible to eat."

A group of dancers left the patio and stood silhouetted between the open French doors. Steven and I found a spot on the floor. David came over and sat next to us.

241

More voices joined in the last chorus of "Lemon Tree." When it was over, everyone clapped and shouted for the boys to go on. They strummed some more chords.

"Where have all the flowers gone?" Tony and Stretch sang together. Softly. "Long time passing. Where have all the flowers gone? Long time ago. Where have all the flowers gone? Young girls picked them, every one. When will they ever learn? When will they ever learn?"

They sang on, through the young girls picking husbands, through the husbands "gone for soldiers, every one," through the soldiers "gone to graveyards, every one," back to "where have all the flowers gone?" And by the time they got to the last chorus, there wasn't a sound in the house. When they ended the song with a loud chord, nobody moved.

Then Tony hit his guitar, and he and Stretch strummed chords loud and fast. Their friends in the room had heard them do this before. They were ready:

"If I had a hammer, I'd hammer in the morning, I'd hammer in the evening all over this land."

Everybody sang:

"I'd hammer at danger, I'd hammer out a warning, I'd hammer out love between my brothers and sisters all over this land.

"If I had a bell, I'd ring it in the morning, I'd ring it in the evening all over this land.

"If I had a song, I'd sing it in the morning . . ."

I've heard this folk song sung a dozen times. It has always moved me. But I never really heard the lyrics before, and I never sang them before. On the last round, I shouted them out with everyone else in the room.

As I did so, I caught sight of our hostess's mother sitting on the floor in the foyer. She was singing, too.

242

*"It's the hammer of justice, it's the bell of freedom,*
*It's the song about love between my brothers and sisters,*
*A-all over this land!"*

Tony and Stretch put their guitars gently down on the couch. To pleas of "More," they shook their heads no. The kids in the doorway moved out on the patio, and the Beatles reigned again. It was midnight.

"Can we go now?" David asked. I nodded. We said good night to Steven and our hostess and her mother, and walked out to the car.

"Hey, would you drop me at Nancy's?" David asked.

"Sure," I said. And I did. "It was a wonderful party," I told him. "I don't think I'll ever forget it."

He nodded, smiled, and waved me off.

I drove back to Bess's dizzy from the profusion of my own thoughts and emotions. I felt so warm and so full and so sad and so amused and so worried and so reassured and so bewildered, and so atavistic.

I staggered to bed.

The next morning I called Gretel. I told her my father had come to take me home. She hardly said a word. She was happy for me. But she was stunned. We said a choked goodbye.

I called David. I had a great deal to thank him for. He thought it was too soon for me to leave. I said I felt I had to go for more reasons than I could articulate. We said goodbye.

I called my husband to ask him to meet me the following day at the airport. He said, "Are you sure?" I said I was. "Then come home," he said. "The house is empty without you."

No words ever meant more to me.

# 23

$G$OODBYE, GRETEL. Thank you. (Bless you.) Goodbye, gang. Goodbye, Bess, David, everybody. Goodbye,
Urban High.

It was over. Over, over, over. Thank heaven.

I slept through my trip back to New York, the sleep of
the shocked. When I got home, I went to bed without
unpacking, unwilling and unable to do anything, particularly talk. After ten days I managed to put two feet on the
floor and eventually I was able to celebrate, a little late,
the occasion of my thirty-fourth birthday. It was months,
though, before I realized that I could laugh safely in
public, and when the realization hit me, I let out the
biggest nonvirginal guffaw you ever heard.

Getting out of Urban had been no more difficult than
getting into it. All I had to do was return my books to the
teachers who had given them to me, and sign out.

I waited until 9:15 A.M., when all my friends would be
in class, took a deep breath, and walked into that mon-

strous structure for the last time. It looked strangely still and empty when everyone was tucked inside. I dreaded having to interrupt classes in session, but there was comfort in the fact that I was leaving; it really didn't matter anymore what Urban saw when it looked at me.

I barely made a ripple. Mr. Goodman said he was sorry to see me go. No one else said anything until I got to Mr. Roth, and he said that no doubt I would be better off in New York. Then he added, nicely, "I don't know what this is all about, but good luck."

My home room teacher, after all those days of ignoring me, at last seemed to take an interest in my welfare. "Oh, you're leaving," she said, as though she cared. "Well, we're sorry to lose you, Lyn. We were just getting to know you."

The registrar's office signed me out and gave me a transfer slip, a small pink document which someday I will frame and hang. For the moment, it remains in a drawer with my other souvenirs of Urban High: a daily class schedule bearing the signatures of my teachers, a bus pass, a student activities card, a school newspaper, a gym suit with bloomers, and a seventy-nine-cent belt, never worn.

My most valuable souvenir, however, is one that can't be either framed or worn. It's the marked change in my attitude toward life. It's the pleasure I take in being myself—in being this adult, this human being. I grew at Urban High, and for a person my size, that's saying a lot.

I'm not sure I learned nearly as much about them as I did about me, but I learned something. I learned that I was wrong in my initial premise that kids today are no different from what they were seventeen years ago. They are different. But I wasn't completely wrong. In many ways, they are the same.

Physically, girls have changed more obviously than boys have. There are more girls who are bigger, built better, healthier-looking, more artfully made up. There are more genuinely beautiful ones, a fact that no doubt rests heavily on the girls who are not beautiful. It is much more difficult today—much sadder, much more complex —to be average-looking. To be homely is more of a tragedy. For both girls and boys, to be average or plain or worse is much more difficult to bear.

There are more kids who have everything, and the gap between them and everybody else has widened enormously. The difference between the super-kids and the other kids is no longer a fine social line, but a cavern. Not to be super is devastating, though it always may have been, I don't know; when I was a real teenager I was one of the super ones. It was possible to be super a teenage generation ago, even though you were short and scrawny and dark-haired, if your parents were middle-class and you made good marks. These are not sufficient qualifications anymore. You must also, today, live in a super suburb, have a car, have charge accounts, have traveled, and be tall and tanned and silky-haired, and cool.

What has not changed about sixteen-year-olds is their essential naïveté, innocence, and idealism. They are children, just as I was a child at their age, though heaven knows I didn't think I was at the time. I was able to get along with Gretel and her friends, I believe, not because I was acting like a teenager but because I was acting like a child.

It is because I found them to be children—by and large kind of dumb, terribly shallow, incomplete, ultimately boring—that I cannot be a party to the current hysteria about the change in teenage morality. I simply do not believe mobile morality is a different problem from the one our parents faced and their parents did before them. I went to beer parties when I was sixteen. At one of them, I recall distinctly, I drank thirteen glasses of beer, chug-a-lug, passed out cold, woke up three hours later and drove home alone—twelve miles—half on the road and half off. At that particular party, too, one of my eight best girl friends—a girl whose virtue I would have sworn for—"went all the way" with the unrequited love of my life. Within a year of that party, she and another of the girls were shotgun brides. That's life.

High school kids today are taking the rap, I believe, for a lot of the highly publicized, kinky activities of college kids. A great percentage of the articles in my file on teenagers in trouble are about eighteen- and nineteen-year-olds, but you wouldn't know so unless you were scratching for that information. A college-age teen is a far different creature from his high school counterparts.

Certainly my friends, the low elevens, showed in their conversations that they knew much more about sex than I did at their age. But are they making use of the knowledge? Are they—let's get to it directly—screwing? I'm sure I would be the heroine of the Western hemisphere if I could say an emphatic "Yes" and finally prove that, just as everybody suspected, the new generation is going straight to hell in plastic wrap. But I can't say it. I don't believe it. Did Gretel go all the way with her ex? Did Angela get laid by the boy with the beard? Did David make it with his girl friend at midnight that Saturday? Who knows?

Sure, I think some of the kids were screwing. About the same percentage that were when I was sixteen. No more, no less, and with just as little sophistication and just as much fear, and for the same reasons: out of curiosity or need or rebellion. I do not believe the kids I met on this crazy trip were freer sexually than the kids I used to know, though, Lord knows, more of them looked as if they

247

were. Even a nine-year-old looks obscene doing the jerk—to anybody who's done the real thing. But she's only dancing. So are most of the sixteen-year-olds.

What really puzzles me is not them but us. I don't understand how we got so old so soon. I can't fathom what turned us into crotchety fuddy-duddies tsk-tsking over the young—so *soon*. I think it's quite possible, though, that I've learned the precise moment one can technically be called old; it's the first time one starts complaining about the sinful behavior of the young.

How did that happen to us old swingers so soon? It was just yesterday that we were asking our own parents, "Weren't you ever young?" Just yesterday that we were saying, "Oh, Mother! For heaven's sake, things are different now!" Just yesterday that we were trying to get out from under a suffocating blanket of old-fashioned morality, trying to get away from the suggestion of evil in boogie-woogie and jitterbugging and—*mercy*—bobby socks. Who would have thought we could get so fusty so soon?

When are we going to break the chain of clucking and headshaking over the young? "I don't know what's the matter with young people today"—1960, 1950, 1940, 1930, 1920, 1910, 1900, name the decade, that's the slogan.

Yes, kids have changed. Yes, they are not precisely what we were. Does that mean they have changed for the worse? If they are not what we were, could they perhaps be an improvement?

I believe they are adapting, in rhythm and size and style, to the world they must live in. They are going to go to the moon. They are going to float in space. They are going to be unbearably crowded. They are going to need different minds and different bodies, and I for one am glad they seem to be getting them. Maybe their kids will grow gills so when the bomb drops they can live under water. Who knows?

Suppose their morality has changed. Suppose they do know more about sex than we knew. Is that necessarily bad? What makes us think we did so well in our day, in our way? If we're so all-fired sound, what is our generation doing lying on analysts' couches, retching up the conflicts of its early years?

Why are we surprised that these teenagers are whatever they are? We look at them and talk about them as though they had sprung full-grown from transistor radios. They are *us*—reflected in a Coney Island mirror. Boomerang. We tossed them out and they came right around and hit us in the back of the head. *Whomp. Thwack.* And *oops.*

I'll tell you what today's teenagers are. They are derivative. They're little distorted carbon copies of Big Daddy and Big Mommy. The only original thing about them is their music. I love that bloody music, that crazy sound of the sixties. When it goes, man, it is the only honest thing on earth. It wails and it whines and it jerks and it pounds, and it's so innocent and sweet and funny and terrible, if you really listen, it could make you cry.

I particularly love it now, after my days with Gretel *et al.*, because it is the only thing about *them* that's not a frightening imitation of *us.* I'd watch them make up and get dressed and talk on the phone and chatter away and pass judgments, and flirt and flutter, and after I got through giggling to myself I wanted to shout at them: "STOP MIMICKING YOUR SUPERIORS! THAT'S NOT NICE!"

This I envy them: their effortless good health, their sheen. Since my bizarre excursion into their world I have an acute sense of pleasure in being my own age. Not in looking it and not in feeling it, but in being it. I don't mind the gray in my hair anymore, but I wish the rest of it were shinier. I wish I didn't have to work so hard at looking well. I wish I weren't getting flabby. Perhaps, though, the lack of tautness in my upper arms is a small price to pay. For what? For potency.

That's what I am that they are not. I am potent. I can make myself felt. I can hold up my hand and say *"Wait a minute!"* I can say *No, I won't* and *Yes, I can.* I can say *This is me.* I am this woman in this house with this man in this small sphere of this large world. This is mine. This small thing. And this. Not much, but mine. See me. I am a person. These are my limitations. These are my potentialities. You may not like me, but that doesn't mean I have to change. I don't have to submit. I don't have to repress. I can pack and go. Or, better yet, I can suggest that you pack and go.

Be young again? Not on your life. Not today. Not in this world where there is so much of everything. How do you get a sense of self in their world of super-beings? What in God's name do you have to do to be an individual? Boy, oh boy . . . good luck to you, David, baby. You've got high hopes and you're all on your own in that crush out there. If you had been in *my* graduating class, you would have been covered with medals. But in your graduating class? I don't know what you can do. And listen, little David, why don't you let your hair grow a bit longer? Because, you see, when you go in the Army you'll have to get a crew cut, which is really most unflattering to the male head. Even if you don't go in the Army and get a crew cut, one day your hair will be thinning quite noticeably and you won't be able to get it to grow down over your ears. Do it now, David.

Be young again? Not me. I've got too much ego. And I know a secret. I know that when you're a teenager, nobody looks at your face. How do I know? Well, you see, this strange think happened to me. I registered in a high school and attended classes disguised as an adolescent, and not one adult—from Dean of Girls to school doctor—noticed. I got away with it. And I came home knowing that though teenagers may be running the economy, controlling the airwaves, taking over the highways, and turning 25,000,000 households inside out, nobody is looking them in the eye. Except when they are alone together, they are in an alien environment, lumped in a mass as though they were a single threatening entity instead of 25,000,000 individual—if only partially formed—human beings, a few million aged thirteen, a few million aged nineteen, and all the rest some age in between.

I have seen their special world, and let me tell you I am not worried about whether today's teenagers are familiar with a dozen intimate positions. I am worried about the kinds of teachers they are exposed to, the kind of environment they go into when they leave home in the morning.

I didn't go to Urban High looking for this worry. I didn't go to a high school to learn about high schools. I went to high school because that's where the kids were. I didn't want to get involved in problems of education. That's for Admiral Rickover. I didn't want to let myself think when I got in the middle of the cafeteria mayhem or heard a political lecture in English class. But I got involved, and now I can't forget the anger and exhaustion I felt at the end of each of my days.

There were a lot of hostile young people at Urban High. Like the kids who made life grim around the hot-dog counter. There were also a lot of passive, washed-out young people. Like Gretel, whose only ambition was to get a fellow, any fellow, and get married and have an identity and ride a downtown bus without hearing "Ugh, teenagers" from the likes of me.

Put down. They are always being put down.

At least in schools like Super High there are mitigating circumstances. There is room to have a long stride, a place to put your elbows. There is light, and air, and cleanliness. There is also motivation for achievement because there is recognition of it. But what's going to become of the kids who can't go to the super-schools? What happens when they can't take one more day of being impotent, each on his own day?

STOP THREATENING ME! That's what I wanted to shout in my classrooms. If you don't cover your book by Wednesday . . . if you don't have your homework written on lined paper . . . if you don't bring your dollar for Student Government . . . if you don't keep quiet . . . if you don't stop . . . if you don't start . . . *you'll be punished.*

Good God, there must be some other way.

Yes, they are passive. Yes, they are zombies. Yes, it is impossible to get a rise out of them in a classroom. Why should it be otherwise? Answer Mr. Roth in some wild, original way. Go ahead, I dare you. No, don't be original, just be wrong. Try it. See how you feel after he wipes up the floor with you.

Good training, you might think. Life is like that. Teaches you to get along with the boss. But there's a difference. A grown man can quit his job without being called a dropout.

We've got special schools for grooming drones. I didn't know. And I don't like knowing, because now Urban High is my responsibility. I could avoid it, but I won't because I have learned that responsibility is a privilege that comes with age. And I am glad to be of age.

Now, then, let me ask it: Do I, probably the only person who has walked among them and lived to tell the tale, understand today's youth? In the language I learned while hiding in their huts, "Unh-unh," which means "not exactly." But I've seen enough of their inner workings to be convinced that they are our children—for better or worse, ours—and not the advance guard of an enemy nation. I am also delighted to be through with them, by the way. Rest assured I am not running around Long Island crashing Sweet Sixteen parties. And don't invite me to any, either, because I won't show.

I do have a few theories about what makes them tick. Yes, I do. But those theories are going to die with me because what I've really learned from this episode is that we should stop trying to understand them. The way I figure it, by the time we do, *they* will be *us*, and we'll find ourselves with a firm grip on our own tails. By that time, too, *they* will have their own younger generation to cluck over, and so on and so on. You don't have to take my word on this, however. Ask your mother.

Would I do it all over if, say, I had to? Now there's a question I've asked myself a few hundred times. I believe the answer I've immediately offered me is an honest one. "Good God, no" is the way I've usually put it. But I'm not sure. Some days I find myself staring in a mirror, squinting, counting lines, and wondering: Could I get away with it again? Could I?

"What do you know about teenagers?" Well, sir, my answer now is "More than I care to." Did I communicate with them? Not really. I watched them and listened to them and thought a lot about what it was to be one of them. Maybe, having come this far with me, you've remembered a bit about being young, yourself. I hope so. I hope this book evoked the past for you as much as the adventure did for me.

I could not wish you more.